The
BBC
Microcomputer
Disk Companion

Tony Latham

Prentice/Hall  **International**

Englewood Cliffs, New Jersey   London   New Delhi   Rio de Janeiro
Singapore   Sydney   Tokyo   Toronto   Wellington

DEDICATION

To the engineers at Acorn Computers Ltd.,
for designing and producing a fine machine.

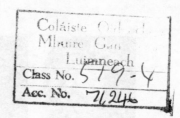
British Library Cataloging in Publication Data

Latham, Tony
The BBC Microcomputer disk companion

1. Data base management   2. BBC Microcomputer
I. Title
001.64'42   QA76.9.D3
ISBN 0-13-069311-1

Library of Congress Cataloging in Publication Data

Latham, Tony, 1936-
The BBC Microcomputer disk companion

Includes index.
1. BBC Microcomputer – Programming.   I. Title.

II. Title: The BBC Microcomputer disk companion
QA76.8.B35L36   1983   001.64'2   83-17753
ISBN 0-13-069311-1

© 1983 by Tony Latham

ISBN 0-13-069311-1

Prentice-Hall International Inc., London
Prentice-Hall of Australia Pty., Ltd., Sydney
Prentice-Hall Canada, Inc., Toronto
Prentice-Hall of India Private Limited, New Delhi
Prentice-Hall of Japan, Inc., Tokyo
Prentice-Hall of Southeast Asia Pte., Ltd., Singapore
Prentice-Hall Inc., Englewood Cliffs, New Jersey
Prentice-Hall Do Brasil Ltda., Rio de Janeiro
Whitehall Books Limited, Wellington, New Zealand

Printed in Great Britain by A.Wheaton & Co. Ltd., Exeter

10 9 8 7 6 5 4

Contents

iii

Acknowledgements

I would like to thank Mike Sein for
assisting with the programs and
articles contained in this book; Acorn
Computers Ltd. and Optimus Graphic
Design Ltd. for the use of the
photograph on page 4; Microware
(London) Ltd. for the use of the
photograph on page 14; and my wife
Iris for her massive effort in typing the
material and for her unfailing support.

Literacy

Long, long ago the magic art was born,
When time was still quite new.
On clay or sand, strange mystic lines were
drawn;
What wonderous lines they drew!

They painted speech, drew laughter, carved
out sighs,
Formed sound within one's head and spoke unto
the eyes.

Could he foresee for one moment, who foolish
'prentice taught;
That his magic would add color and his
lines embody thought?

Could he foresee for one moment, that as
each new soul took part;
They would marvel at his handywork and
embellish more, his art?

Tony.

The
BBC
Microcomputer
Disk Companion

1 Introduction

Eventually, when you tire of waiting for your tapes to load information into your computer and when your purse has recovered from the shock of buying the machine in the first place, you will need this book. By the time this happens you will have gained a little knowledge of terms such as hardware, software and language, but in order to extend this knowledge and prepare you for your next major step in the Microworld, I will endeavor within these pages to explain both what disk drives can do and how the (BBC) microcomputer handles them.

During the last few years, experience with the Computer Users Club has shown that most people buying a computer for domestic purposes, use it for six to eight months before purchasing a disk system. Since the User Guide supplied by 'Acorn' (the Company who created the BBC Computer) is a fairly comprehensive book, a reasonable knowledge of 'Basic' is assumed. A small amount of assembly language will be encountered and is explained later in this book.

The book is structured in a manner that allows you to start using your disk drives at the earliest possible moment, with the more technical details and program

2

examples given in the later chapters. This is done in the knowledge that every person with a new toy would like to get on with it and not sit reading for the best part of a day beforehand.

It may interest you to know that the original of this book was written using a BBC Microcomputer and a pair of double tracking disk drives provided by the publishers, thereby earning my undying gratitude. My thanks are also due to members of the Computer Users Club for their kind co-operation and assistance.

To my certain knowledge there are people in remote corners of the world who already have disk drive units purchased for use with previous equipment. Many schools for example have disk drives on older, less efficient computers which they would like to use with the BBC machine. To do this the disk has to be conditioned, 'Formatted' in a manner that suits the BBC Computer. Our work therefore will satisfy their needs.

The choice of programs given in this book allows the reader who does not have a Formatting Disk to enter the format program manually, format a disk, save the program on the newly formatted disk, then enter and save the Verifier, the Word Processor and the Menu programs which, together with the instructions contained herein form the basis of a Utility Disk with auto start capability.

As far as I am aware this has never been done for any other computer manufactured to date. The usual procedure is for the manufacturer either to sell the formatter separately and, in some cases, at much enhanced prices, or to sell the formatted disk, which means that the user would constantly be re-ordering further supplies, neither situation being entirely satisfactory.

All the programs of course serve in their own way to illustrate the powerful machine operating system routines supplied in the BBC Computer.

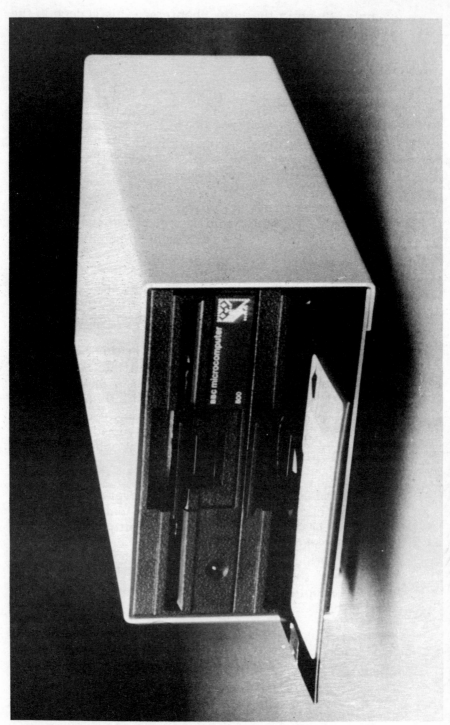

Fig 1.1 The BBC Microcomputer Double Disk Drive

2 Disk Handling

The Choices Available

At this moment in time, the economic mass storage of digital information is achieved by four main techniques.

(a) paper tape;
(b) magnetic tape;
(c) magnetic disk;
(d) bubble memory;

You require one or more of these media if you are to store the programs that you use to conduct your day to day affairs and to store the data that such programs generate. Paper tape is the slowest form of storage. The electro-mechanical method used to punch the holes through the paper dictates the slower pace and at the same time generates quite a lot of noise. The equipment is also bulky and could not be considered suitable for the domestic environment.

Bubble memories on the other hand are silent and very quick, but until such time as the tycoons get their act together, they will remain too expensive for small business or for domestic use.

You will require both the remaining options, for although magnetic tape is too slow and cumbersome for mass data filing purposes, it may be the easiest means of transporting information and programs from machine to machine since not all users can afford disk systems. When time is not important or when the files are not too long the normal tape handling is fine. You will have to hunt for a decent program and most likely you will have to modify a program to suit your own particular needs. It would, under these circumstances, be worth considering endless tape as an alternative.

Disk drives are therefore the answer to low cost mass data handling. All that remains is to look at the types of drive that are available, explain the meaning of terms such as 'head crashes' and the like, then look at how the BBC Microcomputer is designed to handle the drives.

Having decided that you require a disk system, you are now faced with three main options:

(e)   hard disk;
(f)   8 inch (20.3cm) floppy disks;
(g)   floppy disks:

The surface area available on a disk governs the amount of data that can be stored upon it. There are techniques that allow more data to be packed onto a disk surface than that which used to be accepted as 'normal'. Of these, we will be interested in what is known as 80 track format and what is known as double density storage.

The 80-track format is sometimes called double tracking and this should not be confused with double density. I will describe these items in detail later but for the moment wish to confine myself to the do's and don'ts of disk handling.

Let us start by considering a hard disk system. As the name implies, a hard disk consists of a rigid circular plate mounted on a center spindle. The surfaces of the plate are coated with a magnetic layer in much the same way as a normal tape cassette.

Inside a disk drive a device sensitive to magnetism is used to 'read' magnetic codes arranged on a circular disk. The device can also create such codes on the disk surface. This then is called a read/write head, similar to the head of a domestic tape recorder. Often two heads are used, arranged on either side of the disk as shown in Fig. 2.1(a). Usually the disks are stacked in layers, each one with its own pair of heads, the top and bottom of such stacks being protected from dust and damage by a cover plate Fig. 2.1(b). The whole assembly is placed inside a case whose only air supply is drawn through a filter, capable of extracting even smoke from the incoming air.

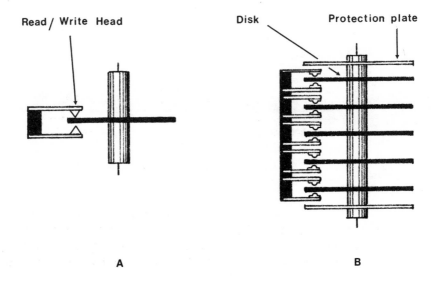

Read / Write Head   Disk   Protection plate

A   B

Fig. 2.1 Typical Hard Disk System

The disks revolve at very high speed and the heads are set extremely close to the disk surface, in fact they float on a cushion of air derived from the aerodynamic shape of the head. This gap, known as the flying height, is often only 100 μinch (2.5μm), where μinch is one millionth part of an inch.

Head Crashes

Fig. 2.2 shows a representation of the relative size of some of the pollutants that could enter the drive system were it not for the filter. Any of these could spoil the airflow supporting the head, causing the head to crash into the disk surface at 100 mph (160Kph) or similar speeds. The result of this type of collision can be imagined, apart from the loss of valuable data, the cost of a new 'platter' (disk) for this type of drive is around $100.

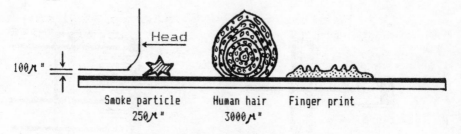

Fig. 2.2 Pollutants

The quality control on this type of drive however, allows the manufacturers to give a three-year guarantee of 100% error-free handling. The typical storage capability of a hard disk stack is between 5 and 10 million bytes - a byte being 8 bits of information and a bit being in effect an electrical impulse.

The cost of these systems as you can imagine is high and the use of modern technology is enabling the production of floppy disks (flexible platters) that have similar storage densities to those of hard disks, but whose cost is only a fraction of the hard disk prices. On good quality floppy disk drives, the read/write heads are in contact with the surface of the disk and the term 'head crash' loses its meaning.

Although it is not important that you understand the internal working of a drive unit, the following description is included to satisfy your curiosity. What happens is this. The operator opens the access door on the front of the unit and inserts a floppy disk into the drive. During this action a metal clamshell assembly (see Fig. 2.3) removes the head from the path of the disk. When the door is closed, the cone, which is mounted on the clamshell, automatically centers and 'clamps' the disk to the drive spindle. During this time a device called the head load solenoid prevents the read/write heads from touching the disk. This is known as the 'unloaded' position.

When the drive is activated, the solenoid loads the heads onto the disk to a precise pressure, thus extending the life of the disk. Drive units that do not contain a head load device can suffer from a greater degree of head and disk wear. The head load solenoid is also used to remove the heads from the disk during the period of time when the drive motor is on, but the transfer of data is not required. Pollution of the disk surface can still be the cause of data loss and disk errors, and the following section outlines some of the points that you should observe in order to minimize such corruption.

Fig. 2.4 shows a typical disk. It consists of a thin circle of mylar, coated on both sides with a mixture of magnetic oxides and a lubricating medium. It is contained within a black card case from which it is never removed. The case contains a window through which the head reads the disk and a central hole through which the drive clamps onto the hub of the disk.

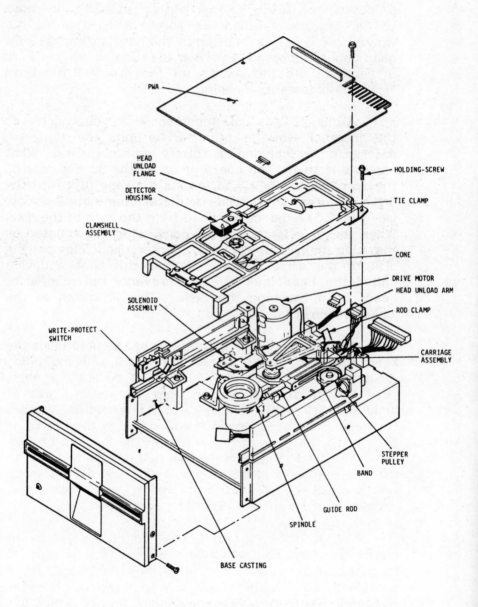

PWA

HEAD
UNLOAD
FLANGE

DETECTOR
HOUSING

CLAMSHELL
ASSEMBLY

SOLENOID
ASSEMBLY

WRITE-PROTECT
SWITCH

HOLDING-SCREW

TIE CLAMP

CONE

DRIVE MOTOR
HEAD UNLOAD ARM

ROD CLAMP

CARRIAGE
ASSEMBLY

STEPPER
PULLEY

BAND

GUIDE ROD

SPINDLE

BASE CASTING

Fig. 2.3 An Exploded View of a Typical Floppy Disk Drive

In the top edge of the case is a small square slot called a 'write protection notch' which, if covered by an adhesive tab, will prevent any further data from being recorded onto the disk. Removal of the adhesive tab where fitted, allows data to be written onto the disk as required.

On one side of the case there is usually a label with an arrow on it to indicate the direction of insertion into the drive.

At the time of inserting the disk the write protection notch should face towards the LED (light emitting diode) visible on the front of the drive unit. The LED is on whenever the drive is active. If the drive does not have a light emitting diode, then the label on the disk is usually facing upwards, or if the drive is mounted vertically the label is usually facing to the right hand side of the drive, with the protection notch uppermost. As a point of interest, on an 8 inch (20cm) floppy disk the notch should be uncovered for write protection, this being the opposite of a 5.25 inch disk.

The disks are usually sold in boxes of 10 with the labels and the write protection tabs included in the box.

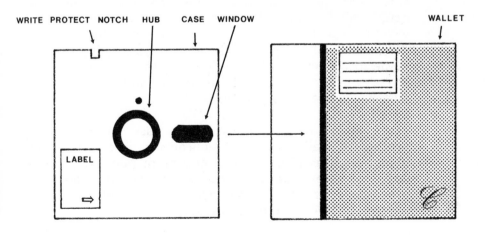

Fig. 2.4 Typical Disk

BMDC - B

To insert a disk into the drive unit, open the access door on the front of the drive. The drive should be switched on at the mains, or if powered by the computer, the computer should already be on. It is not desirable to turn the power to the drive unit either on or off whilst a disk is inside the machine, for the initial surge of power could damage the program or data on that disk.

Holding the disk by the edge of the case containing the label ensure that the write protection notch, see Fig. 2.4, is on the side nearest to the little lamp (LED). Insert the window edge (see Fig. 2.4) into the slot and press gently until the disk is inside the drive. Close the access door. On no account should any force be used. Bending the disk or trapping it in the access door could cause damage.

Protection and Care of Disks

Nicotine and dust are the main contamination affecting disk drives within a domestic environment. In the same way that these two substances discolor the walls of your home and the windows on the inside of your car, they coat the head with a thin film and reduce its effectiveness. Magnetic fields caused by electrical equipment, mainly due to the transformers contained within such devices, can erase the data from a floppy disk. The oils from the surface of your skin, should it come into contact with the disk surface, will be carried on to the heads and cause a film to which nicotine and dust will more readily adhere.

Never write on the disk case or on to the protective wallet whilst it contains a disk with a sharp object such as a pencil or a ball point pen. If you must write on the case then use a felt-tip pen and light pressure. It is recommended that labels should be written before sticking them onto the disk.

Keep the access doors shut when the drives are not in use.

Replace any disk not in use into its wallet and also into a dust free container. Do not leave them lying around on top of equipment. The following list summarizes the points made above.

1.	Avoid smoking whilst working with disk units.

2.	Avoid magnetic fields.

3.	Do not touch the surface of the disk.

4.	Do not write on the disk case other than with a felt tip pen.

5.	Replace all protective covers.

6.	Keep access doors closed.

7.	Keep disks away from sources of heat i.e. radiators and window sills.

Posting Disks

There is bound to be a time when you require the services of the postal authorities to transport a disk for you. The packaging of the disk in a good stout container is obvious to all, but less noticeable is the fact that the postal services of most countries utilize the 'electric' railway or underground service for part of the journey. The motor units of this service all produce electrical fields which will quite effectively wipe a disk clean.

To counter this, make a cardboard folder to contain the disk and prevent bending damage. Then wrap the whole lot in kitchen foil prior to applying the outside packaging. As an alternative a tin box can be used but the postal charge will be higher.

Fig. 2.5 Single and Double Disk Drive Units

Floppy Disk Drive Units

Floppy disk drive units are supplied either as a single drive or as a pair of drives mounted in one case together with a power supply. They are known as single-drive or double-drive units see Fig. 2.5. The drives which have only one head and read only one surface of the disk are known as single-sided drives, whilst those with two heads which can read both sides, are known as double-sided drives. You can see from this that you may buy a double-sided single drive or a single-sided double drive or any permutation you care to envisage.

To make matters worse, the data is stored on the disk on concentric circles called 'tracks' of which there are 40 per side. We will study this aspect later but, for the moment, you should understand that for some reason best known to the creator of all this double talk, the 40-track drives are known as single tracking. Drives can also be obtained that have 80 tracks per side and are of course known as double tracking.

There are various methods of using abbreviations to convey the above information, e.g. DDD, SDS, etc. For the beginner these could cause confusion, so throughout this book the following abbreviations will be used.

[D] = double [S] = single [t] = tracking
[s] = sided [d] = drive

If two drives are placed one above the other the top drive is referred to as drive 0 and the bottom one as drive 1. The double drive unit shown in Fig. 2.5 would have the left-hand drive as drive 0 and the right-hand drive as drive 1. These numbers in fact should be seen as referring to the read/write heads contained within the drive, for on [DsDd] units the left-hand unit is drive 0 and the reverse side of the disk is drive 2. The right-hand unit is drive 1, the reverse of the disk being drive 3. It is important that you understand these distinctions, and they are logical, although not at first sight.

When you first apply power to your computer, or after every press of the BREAK key, drive 0 is selected automatically. This is known as selection by default. You may have asked the computer to make drive 3 the currently selected drive, but if you press BREAK you default back to drive 0.

This effect can be used to your advantage. Consider a write protected disk containing programs for business purposes, placed in drive 0, and a disk placed in drive 1 on which the data is to be stored after handling by the chosen program. The program itself dictates that drive 1 be used for all read and write purposes. If anything goes wrong, then the computer defaults and cannot write on the protected disks, thus protecting the data and the programs.

Before a brand new disk can be used it must be formatted. Formatting will be explained more fully later in the book. Briefly it consists of dividing the disk into concentric tracks (either 40 or 80 per disk side). The tracks are further subdivided into blocks called sectors, each sector being capable of holding 256 bytes. When information is recorded onto the disk, the first two sectors of the first track are used by the computer to store information whereby it can relocate the information at a later date. This special area is called a catalog. In order to format you require a utilities disk on which you will find a format program and a verify program. If you do not have a utilities disk you will require a 'formatted' disk before you are able to save any of your programs.

A formatting program is included later in this book for the benefit of those people desirous of using their own drives. This should be typed into the computer, used to format a disk and then saved onto the formatted disk and kept for future use.

The disk drive units are connected to the computer by a 34-way flat ribbon cable which usually has a coloured 'tracer' down one edge. The edge with the tracer is on the right hand side when the lead is plugged into the computer, see Fig. 2.6. The ribbon cable should be pushed onto the plug gently but firmly until the connector clamps at either end clip onto the plug.

If the drive is to be supplied with voltages from the computer, a second lead connects to the plug on the power supply of the computer. The connections should be made with the Mains switched off. Insert the polarized plug (polarized means that the plug will only fit the socket one way) into the socket supplied underneath the left hand side of the computer. The socket is marked Auxiliary Power Output. Since the BBC Computer supply will only provide 1.25 Amperes at 12 Volts and 5 Volts dual drive units should have their own stabilized power source.

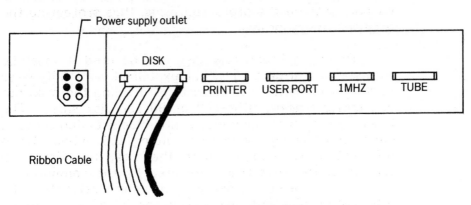

Fig. 2.6 Disk Outlet Connections

Formatting a Disk

A 'formatted' disk is required before a disk system can be used to store programs or information. The following pages describe briefly how to format a disk. Later in the book formatting is explained in greater detail, but at this point the intent is simply to create a formatted disk which can be used to try out the commands we are about to discuss. The reader who possesses a formatting disk should turn to the next page, whilst those who do not possess a formatting disk can create one by typing in the format program as listed in Chapter Seven. To type in the listing and correct any errors introduced by such typing requires some knowledge of 'Basic' and this is assumed since the User Guide supplied with the BBC machine is quite a good book. The dialog given below allows the reader to create a formatting disk using the format program.

Type in the format program.

In the examples which follow the computer will be asking questions, each question being terminated by a question mark (?). Any characters after the question mark should be read as 'your response' to the question which you enter then press the key marked RETURN. The RETURN key tells the computer to process your entry and move on to the next stage of the program. All entries from the keyboard finish with return, unless the computer arranges otherwise.

Type RUN (RETURN)

DRIVE NO.? 0 (RETURN)

REMOVE FORMAT DISK (ignore in this instance)

Insert blank disk into drive 0.

NO. OF TRACKS REQUIRED (80,40,35)?(as required to suit the drive used)

READY TO FORMAT DRIVE (Y/N)? Y(RETURN)
(when the disk is formatted)

FORMAT ANOTHER DISK (Y/N)? N(RETURN)

You would now type in the following, in order to save the program on the newly formatted disk, if required.

SAVE "A.FORMAT" (RETURN)
*TITLE UTILITY-40(or 80)(RETURN)

From now on you can run the formatter with CHAIN "A.FORMAT", or later, in conjunction with a menu program by selection of a single letter.

The VERIFY program, given at the back of the book, can then be entered and saved ready for use later by employing: SAVE "A.VERIFY"(RETURN).

The utility disk supplied by Acorn Ltd. does the same job as the formatter already mentioned but is handled in a slightly different manner.

Ensure that the write protection notch on the utilities disk is covered by one of the small tabs provided, since this will prevent the accidental erasure of the information contained on the disk. <u>Insert the utilities</u> disk into drive 0.

If 8 inch (20cm) drives are being used, ensure that the notch is without a tab.

Single-sided, Single-tracking, Single drives

(Commands are in capital letters and should be followed by pressing the RETURN key)

*FORM40 0
(Note the space between the numbers 40 and 0)

The computer will respond with

Do you really want to format drive 0?

<u>Remove the format disk and insert the blank disk.</u>

Now enter Y for (Yes). The formatting will proceed and when complete you will see

Do you wish to format again Y/N?

Type N

Single-sided, Single-tracking, Double drives

The dialog runs as follows

*FORM40 1   (= Format drive 1)

Do you really want to format drive 1?

Y

Do you wish to format again?

N

Double-sided, Double-tracking, Single drives

Operate as for [SsStSd] but use *FORM80. The dialog with the computer will guide the proceedings. Be sure not to mix the two disks.

When side 0 is complete, use *FORM80 2 for the second side or reply to the prompt with Y and to 'Which drive?' with 2.

Double-sided, Double-tracking, Double drives

*FORM80 1

Do you really want to format drive 1?

Y

Do you wish to format again Y/N?

Y

Which drive? 3

Do you really want to format drive 3?...etc.

If you wish to format the entire box of disks, it is easier to format all one side first, e.g.

Do you wish to format again Y/N?

(insert new disk)

Y

After which all the obverse (reverse) sides can be handled. Should you prefer to complete each disk in turn, you can program the red user keys to change drives for you as:

```
*KEY 1"*FORM80 1 |M"
*KEY 3"*FORM80 3 |M"
```

The red 'user' key f1 will now allow you to format drive 1 and key f3 will, when pressed, allow drive 3 to be formatted. The appropriate key will now format the drive. The '|M' is the BBC Computer's way of accepting a programmed RETURN key press.

A disk which is new and unformatted is often referred to as a blank disk, whilst a formatted disk which contains no programs is referred to as a formatted blank.

Formatting a disk containing programs which are no longer required produces a formatted blank.

The BBC Microcomputer will handle a wide variety of floppy disk drives but seems to respond best to those drives whose track-to-track search time is less than 20/ms (milliseconds). The older type of drive, used before stepper motors became available, employed a screw drive to position the read/write head over the track and the time taken, being typically 40 ms, is too slow.

Adjustments can be made to various 'link' options on the printed circuit board inside the computer to select 8 inch (20cm) or 5.25 inch (13cm) drives and to select the 4 - 6 ms track-to-track search time most appropriate to the type of drive to be used.

Details of these options can be found in Chapter Seven which covers technical information.

Tracks and formatting are covered more fully in Chapter Six.

Transferring your Programs from Tape to Disk

When the computer is first switched on the words SAVE or LOAD both operate the disk system. These words are explained later. Save or Load from a cassette tape recorder requires the user to change the filing system from disk to tape using *TAPE. Once changed, the filing system can be changed back to disk filing using *DISK. The operations which follow describe the transfer of Basic programs from tape to disk filing systems.

Since you will probably wish to transfer all your programs from tape to disk at one go, it is easier to set the user keys to change between the filing systems.

```
*KEY 0"*TAPE  ¦M"
*KEY 1"*DISK   ¦M"
```

Press BREAK, f0. The tape can now be loaded in the manner described in the User Guide supplied with the computer. Insert the disk into drive 0, for we will be using the default drive to save the programs. *DISK changes the filing system to disk and if you wish to use a drive other than 0, you will need to specify which drive i.e.

```
*KEY 1"*DISK  ¦M   :   *DRIVE 2 ¦M  "
```

The key prints the string both onto the screen and into the input buffer. The '*' forces the operating system to accept valid commands and the colon between the commands allows the string to be treated as a multi-statement line. But, before we start, perhaps you should understand a little about catalogs, filenames and file directories.

When using the BBC Computer in its cassette mode, programs are placed at a lower address (3584(&E00)) than that chosen by machines fitted for disk (6400(&1900)). The reason for this is that memory area below &1900 is used as disk workspace. Where you possess long programs which will no longer run due to insufficient memory, the computer can be returned to its 0.1 state by entering the following two lines:

FOR PROG% = PAGE TO TOP: ?(PROG%-2816)=?PROG% : NEXT

PAGE = &E00 ¦M OLD ¦M *TAPE ¦M

The pointer which tells the computer where to find the start of the program is reset by OLD after the ¦M which means RETURN. As you can see, the FOR NEXT loop moves the program down in memory and alters the value of page. The lines can of course be given line numbers and used at the start of a program if required.

The Catalog

Whenever you save a program onto a formatted disk a small section of track 00 is used to keep a record of the file name. This record also contains numeric details as to where the head should move to, in order to find the file the next time you wish to use it. This record is called the Catalog. The Catalog can hold 31 filenames. It can be placed onto the screen from the currently used drive by typing *. or from a non-selected drive by *.(Drive No.) e.g.

    *.1

gives the catalog of drive 1 even if drive 0 is in current use.

Filenames

A filename is a name given by the user to define the
program, e.g. SAVE "MYPROG" where MYPROG is the
name of the program. On a disk system a filename can
only contain 7 letters or numbers. Spaces are not
allowed within a filename and the symbols : . # $ *   all
have special meanings and should not be used within the
name. A filename should not start with a number. Tape
filing systems use filenames that can contain 10
characters. The other restrictions mentioned above
apply also to tape filenames.

As you can see from this, filenames will probably
have to be changed to a shortened version when
transferring programs from tape to disk. Care should be
taken concerning the choice of name, for if a file called
DEFEND was saved on a disk and a further section of the
same program called defend (lower case letters) was also
saved on the same side of the same disk in the same
directory, then the last entry would overwrite the
original entry. A filename is thus in its most versatile
form when it is composed from a six letter descriptive
name, plus a number i.e. Defend1, Defend2 etc.

Directories and File Specifications

The Catalog can be sub-divided into sections called
Directories, each being represented by a character A to
Z. Directories will be described in full later in the book.
They are shown here as a letter followed by a period '.' to
show that a filename of 7 characters can be extended in
a manner which allows the same name to be used in
different sections of the Catalog e.g.

A.Defend1   B.Defend1

When a program is placed onto the disk using a filename without a directory letter, the computer assumes $. to be the directory. $. is said to be the default directory. Further to this, if a program is placed onto the disk where no choice of drive is given, the computer assumes that the last selection of drive using *DRIVE (Drive number) should also be the drive to use this time. If a drive was not previously selected the computer assumes drive 0 (the left hand or a single drive).

To place the program onto a particular drive requires :(drive number). e.g.

:1.A.Defend1

This is known as a file specification (fsp).

Files may be loaded using their (fsp) and saved using a new name, on a different drive, in a different directory. Where this option is open to you, you are said to be using an ALTERNATIVE FILE SPECIFICATION shown as (afsp). (afsp) can of course be the same as the original (fsp) but overwrite occurs if the file is not protected.

Now we are ready to transfer the tape programs.

*TAPE	(or f0 if defined)
LOAD "Filename"	(or LOAD"" if the next available tape program)

when loading is complete

*DISK	(or f1 if defined)
SAVE (afsp)	

Programs saved in error may be deleted by *DELETE (fsp).

Provision is also made for protecting a particular file from being overwritten by SAVE, *SAVE, *DELETE, *RENAME and *DESTROY commands. These commands will be described in the next chapter.

The file can be 'locked' using the command

*ACCESS(afsp) L

This command is fully described in the next chapter.

3" Microdrives

3" drives handle in exactly the same way as 5.25" drives as far as the BBC Microcomputer is concerned. The amount of available storage is the same. With these drives it is possible to protect one surface and still write to the obverse which can prove a useful feature. The cassettes are rigid and better protected against damage than is possible with a 5.25" or 8" drive.

On the debit side, most program material currently available is on 5.25" disks and these are not readable by the user of a 3" system.

3 Disk Filing System Commands

All your programs should now be on the disk and the next step is to make a backup copy just in case the dog or your children get hold of the original. The Disk File System (DFS) contains some very useful features.

Type *HELP (minimum abbreviation *H.)

> The response from the DFS is:
>
> DFS (Version number)
>
> DFS
> UTILS
> OS (Version number) (OS = Operating System)

Type *HELP DFS

> The response is:
>
> ACCESS (afsp) (L)
> BACKUP (src drv)(dest drv)
> COMPACT (drv)
> COPY (src drv)(dest drv)(afsp)

27

DELETE (fsp)
DESTROY (afsp)
DIR (dir)
DRIVE (drv)
ENABLE
INFO (afsp)
LIB (dir)
RENAME (old fsp)(new fsp)
TITLE (title)
WIPE (afsp)
OS (version number)

The mnemonics are explained below:

(afsp)	=	alternative file specification
(fsp)	=	file specification
(dir)	=	directory letter
(drv)	=	drive number
(src)	=	source
(dest)	=	destination
(L)	=	locked

All of the commands listed above require * before the command word in order to use them. Each of the command words has a minimum abbreviation which will be shown contained inside the square brackets, i.e. [*A.].

   *. used on its own will supply a catalog from the currently selected drive onto the screen. It can also be used after a command which extends the capability of the command to act on more than one filename at a time, i.e.

   *INFO *.$.*

will supply information on all files in directory $.

   *INFO *.*

will supply information for the complete catalog of files.

When *. is used in this way you are said to be using a 'Wildcard'. The term 'Wildcard' originates in the card game 'Poker' where cards numbered 2 are sometimes allowed to represent any other card (deuces wild).

The final * at the end of the command replaces any group of characters. The symbol # may also be used to replace a single character within a wildcard configuration.

Before DFS commands are explained, it should be pointed out that the commands listed in the User Guide supplied with the BBC Microcomputer covering LOAD, SAVE, CHAIN, SPOOL as applied to tape recorders, still apply for disk use. These commands are explained later in this and the following Chapter.

As with the cassette filing system and operating system commands when used within numbered program lines, all * commands should be placed at the end of the line or on a line of their own - otherwise anything following the command on the same line will be ignored.

ACCESS (afsp)(L)
　　[*A.]

If a file is LOCKED the re-use of the (fsp) is prevented. You are able to load a locked file but cannot save again unless with an (afsp). ACCESS is used to both lock and unlock the files. Note the space between the filename and 'L'.

```
*ACCESS Diary3 L   (will lock Diary 3)
*A.Diary3          (will unlock Diary 3)
*A.*.$.*           (would access all files
                    in directory $)
```

The whole disk, if access locked, can be unlocked using *A.*.*

A locked file prevents the use of such commands as *SAVE, *DELETE, *WIPE, *RENAME, and *DESTROY. If the disk is also write protected, *ACCESS itself will produce the error message

DISK WRITE PROTECTED

However, a locked file can be damaged if you reformat that drive accidentally or *BACKUP to that drive with the wrong disk inserted. You must guard against such mishap by placing a write protection tab over the write protection notch on the disk.

*BACKUP (src drv)(dest drv)
    [*BAC.]

This command, in conjunction with the command *ENABLE, is used to duplicate a disk with files by copying every single file from one disk onto another.

The backup can damage locked files if you mix up the disks and will also overwrite material already on the destination disk.   To prevent this, the program is given a double command to ensure that you know what you are doing. To add to a disk containing other material see *COPY.

                    *ENABLE
                    *BACKUP 0 1

will produce a copy of the disk in drive 0 onto the disk in drive 1. Where only one drive is available use *BACKUP 0 0. The program will ask you to insert the source and destination disks into the drive as required. Take care to prevent the two disks from getting mixed up, for if the source disk were blank this would be transferred to the disk which you had hoped to copy onto. The contents of the memory are also altered by this command, so save any valuable material before making a backup disk.

When a switch option is fitted (see end of chapter), which converts an 80-track drive into a 40-track drive, it is not possible to use 'Backup' to create an 80-track from a 40 using two drives with 0 switched to 40, or vice versa.

The conversion is possible however, with such switching arranged, by using *COPY, e.g.

    *COPY 01 *.$.*
  (or *.(DIR).*) should be used as required.
    *TITLE (title)
    *OPT 4 3

COPY (src dr)(dest dr).* will copy all files from one disk to another regardless of directory and without destroying existing files on the destination disk. The *OPT will be more fully explained later.

Where the *OPT and Title are set as required for auto boot purposes, the copy will not transfer these items, whereas BACKUP would. BACKUP will however transfer the information which tells the computer that it is a 40-track not 80-track disk.

*COMPACT (drv)
  [*COM.]

Eventually a point will be reached when the disk surface upon which the programs are being saved is full. At that point the computer responds with an error message:

    (Number &C6) DISK FULL.

There are probably quite a few bits of unused space scattered around the disk, left behind from where programs have been deleted. The error message simply means that none of these sections is long enough to accept the program. *COMPACT moves all the files to the start of the disk, leaving all the spare space as one long continuous block at the end.

It may well be that such an error message could cause a problem with your own program, for example if you were trying to save an array from within your program. To escape and compact would be out of the question, for you would lose the array. In this event error trapping is required.

The error number is given to the variable ERR and the technique goes something like this:

```
100 ON ERROR GOTO 4000
(Then the program continues until)
4000 IF ERR=17THEN END
4010 IF ERR <> &C6 THEN ZZZ ELSE
     *COMPACT
4020 ON ERROR GOTO 4030:GOTO 110:REM
     Try again now
4030 IF ERR<>&C6 THEN ZZZ ELSE *DRIVE
     (X+2)
4040 GOTO 110
```

Given X = current drive and ZZZ = alternative error handling.

As can be seen, if after *COMPACT there is still insufficient room, arrangements can be made to use another disk surface as an alternative. Error 17 = the ESCAPE key.

*COPY (src drv)(dest drv)(afsp)
[*COPY.]

Will copy named files from one disk drive to another e.g.

*COPY 0 1 Text2

Note that no quotation marks are required on the filename, in this case Text2. If a whole series of programs all beginning with, say HA (series of versions of a developing program all with different version numbers) requires copying, then use:

COPY (src drv)(dest drv).HA*

Memory will be affected by *COPY and programs or data held in RAM should be saved prior to using the command. Where *BACKUP would overwrite, *COPY will add to what is already on the disk. A whole directory can be transferred, e.g.

*COPY 0 1 *.A.*

The whole disk can be copies with *COPY

The whole disk can be copies with *COPY (src drv)(dest drv)*.* but the disk catalog information would not be copied and may require direct commands to the destination disk to set this as required (see *TITLE and *OPT).

*DELETE (fsp)
[*DEL.]

The command acts on the currently selected drive and will delete a single specified line.

    *DELETE Text3

It can be seen that it is very easy to delete a file, therefore the command should be used with caution.

*DESTROY (afsp)
[*DES.]

The command is used to delete a series of programs all with the same starting letters to their filenames. It will not clear locked files. Once destroyed the filenames cannot be restored.

    *ENABLE
    *DESTROY *.HA*

The computer will respond by presenting a list of files such as HANGMAN and will ask:

    DELETE Y/N?

Typing "Y" will then delete the files.

The whole disk can be cleared with:

    *ENABLE
    DES..*

*DIR (dir)
[*DI.]

The directory is described on Page 24. This

command allows the user to change the current directory to a different one defined by an alphabetic character (A to Z). For example if 'G' were set the programs saved thereafter would read as G.(fsp) in the catalog. The default directory after BREAK is pressed is always set to $ (pronounced 'string'). Any symbols can be used except *.:!?#

        *DIR A (sets directory A)

*DRIVE (drv)
    [*DR.]

Changes the current drive to the one specified with all new commands working on that drive. Break will reset drive 0. A full description of the drive numbering can be found on Page 16.

        *DRIVE 2 (sets drive 2 to be selected)

*ENABLE
    [*EN.]

To prevent accidental use of disk system commands where those commands can produce irreversible effects *ENABLE is required immediately before the command word. It is required before *BACKUP and *DESTROY.

        *ENABLE
        *BACKUP 0 1

*INFO (afsp)
    [*I.]

Provides numeric information in addition to the information given by a normal catalog (*CAT) as below. A block of files can be listed using *.(XX)* where XX = start letter of the group.

The load address represents the beginning area of memory used by the computer to contain a program fetched from the disk. FF1900 is the start address of memory for normal Basic programs. The execution address represents the point from which the program begins to run, after which a value for length of program is given. Start refers to an area on the disk called a sector which will be described more fully later. In this context it is the sector that the file commences from (the start sector of the file).

*INFO B.INVOICE

(DIR)(FSP)(ACCESS) Load   Execution Length Start
                    Address Address

B. INVOICE   L   FF1900   FF801F   0010C3   00C

*INFO *.B.* also applies to all files in directory B. The INFO on all the catalog will be given with *I.*.* See also *OPT.

*LIB (:(drv).)(dir)
[None]

A library file is one which contains a machine code routine which can be used by a number of other programs contained as separate files. This is a way of saving program size if programs all need the same routines. The library file is accessed like an operating system command by using *(filename).

The command is arranged to set the library to the specified drive and directory. It is used as a pointer to the files which may be acted upon by either the programs in the default drive, or by *(fsp) where (fsp) is a machine code program.

*LIB : 1.D Sets the library on drive 0 to 1.D.

Nothing happens when you enter the command but the 1.D will be added at the time of the next access. To verify this enter *. after setting the library as described above.

Headings will now be shown as:

```
1 <title> (28)
DRIVE 0            Option 0 (off)
Directory :0.$     Library :1.D
```

(List of files)

The library is clearly set to drive 1.D. The idea is that if you type in a *(filename) drive 1 will be searched for any machine code program by that name, which if found will be loaded into the machine and run. The library command extends the search, directing it to another drive and directory, the arrangement being such that a program in the default drive can act in conjunction with a program from the specified library with the drive indicated.

For example:

*FORM40 and *FORM80 which are machine code formatting programs created by Acorn Computers may be run from drive 0 since the library by default (on power-up) is selected as drive 0, directory $.

*RENAME (old fsp)(new fsp)

A file may be renamed and moved to another directory if required using this command. In the example given below a file HANG in directory G will be renamed to HANGMAN in directory E. Files cannot be moved from one drive to another with the RENAME command. Locked files cannot be renamed nor can renaming take place if the disk is write protected. If a file already exists bearing the new fsp, then an error message 'file exists' is given and renaming is aborted.

*RENAME G.HANG E. HANGMAN

*TITLE (disk name)
[*TI.]

Each disk may be given a title containing up to 12 letters which is written after the command. The name is offered inside quotation marks if the name contains a space. Spaces are counted as one letter and where the title is less than 12 characters long, spaces are added to the end of the string by the command. Any characters after the first 12 are ignored and no error messages are produced on this account.

*TITLE "GAMES DISK"

*WIPE (afsp)
[*WI.]

Has the effect of removing files and re-arranging the catalogue. The program asks for confirmation before actually deleting the files. Blocks of files with the same starting letters can be deleted using *WIPE*.XX*

When XX are the starting letters, i.e. HA etc. the computer responds G. HANGMAN, and at this stage deletion takes place if the user enters 'Y'; otherwise the file remains intact. Locked files are not affected by WIPE.

WIPE..* wipes the entire disk leaving only the information on the disk as applied to a formatted blank, together with any title or options previously set.

We will now list the 'Utilities' which are a set of general purpose routines, then explain them, after which we will examine the use of these facilities in connection with actual programs.

Type *HELP UTILS

the response being: DFS (version number)

BUILD (fsp)
DISK
DUMP (fsp)
LIST (fsp)
TYPE (fsp)
OS (version number)

Note: the disk filing system uses the British spelling DISC for DISK on the display. In practice both spellings are accepted as commands.

*BUILD (fsp)
[*BU.]

This command is provided to allow you to construct a file consisting purely of text as opposed to a Basic program or data. One main application of this is word processing.

It is possible using the command to build an ASCII file similar to the *EXEC files or !Boot files which will be described later. The named file is opened and the material entered from the keyboard will be placed into the file. Once the file is open, line numbers are displayed for your entries. To close or finish the file the last entry will be the ESCAPE key e.g.

```
*BUILD TEST
1 First entry
2 Second entry
3 etc.
4 (Esc)
```

The line increments by one and ESC closes the file. SHIFT and a red function key pressed together allows color to be added to the text.

*DISK

The command changes the filing system from tape to disk. The power up or break defaults to disk filing when the DFS chip is included in a Model B computer. *DISC is also accepted as an alternative spelling.

*DUMP (fsp)
　[*DU.]

This produces a Hex listing onto the screen, with ASCII equivalents printed on the righthand side. Since the list scrolls very quickly it is wise to enter page mode, using CTRL/N prior to *DUMP (fsp). Page mode stops the list after each screenful and waits until you press the SHIFT key to allow loading to continue with the next page.

CTRL/O turns off the page mode. Note that I have seen this command not responding to the SHIFT key on a 1.0 MOS system. In later versions of the operating system this appears to have been corrected.

*LIST (fsp)
　[None]

Displays the file on screen in the normal manner covered by the User Guide. Again CTRL/N should be used prior to the command to set page mode listing. The listing uses ASCII characters with each line numbered. However, I have seen this command in difficulties on a 1.0 MOS system.

Listings of Basic programs yield nonsense. The listing and dump are mainly for use on spooled programs which are fetched direct from disk to screen memory only. Therefore corrections cannot be done in the usual manner, using the arrow keys and the 'copy' key.

*TYPE (fsp)
　[*TY.]

Displays text files onto the screen without line numbers. If Basic programs are called as the fsp then nonsense will be displayed. Text files are best viewed by entering page mode (CTRL/N). Difficulty may arise in outputting such text to a printer other than by screen dump, especially if embedded commands are required within the text data which invoke special paper movements or characters.

Normal scrolling i.e. paged mode off can be obtained using CTRL/O.

Text files are in effect ASCII lists. Therefore see also *LIST and *DUMP.

In the paged mode, a new screen full will be displayed each time the SHIFT key is depressed, until the end of the file is reached.

Other Commands

The remaining commands all operate on the disks although they are not all part of the DFS. Some are handled by the language ROM as normal Basic commands, whilst others, usually starting with '*' are accepted by the Machine Operating System (MOS). #:!*. are all treated as special symbols.

*HELP
[*H.]

This is known as a keyword, whose action is as described by Page 27 onwards. This is a Machine Operating System command, not part of the DFS.

HASH (#)

Hash may be used in a 'Wildcard' situation to replace any individual letter, e.g.

*INFO *.D#*

would display information on any file whose first letter in the filename is 'D'.

*CAT (drv)
[*.]

Causes the catalog of a disk to be displayed with *. being the currently selected drive.

*.1 produces the catalog of drive 1 even if the currently selected drive is 0.

Drive numbers 0 to 3 are accepted but any other numbers produce error messages.

When *. is used in conjunction with other DFS commands, it may be regarded as a 'Wildcard', i.e.

INFO.* will display INFO of all files contained on the disk.

*EXEC (fsp)
[*E.]

This command is used to read the contents of the file and treat it as if it were characters being typed at the keyboard. This means that if the contents were a numbered Basic program, (i.e. created using the *SPOOL command to save the Basic instructions in ASCII codes) then these lines of Basic could be added to an existing Basic program already held in the computer RAM area.

*EXEC as applied to tape or disk files created using the *SPOOL command (see later) loads an ASCII Basic file into the computer. If the line numbers coincide with the line numbers of a program already in memory, then that program is overwritten.

If the line numbers are higher, then the incoming program is added to the existing program. Of course RENUMBER [REN.] can be used to condition the program line numbers to suit your purpose.

One point to watch is, if you load a *EXEC file onto your own program to try it i.e. adding a screen dump by *EXEC to a graphics program, you will not then be able to respool the tested program without first dropping the graphics section that has become attached to it. Failure to do this means that the program now has low line numbers added which would overwrite anything in memory when next you use the *EXEC routine. *EXEC is a Machine Operating System command (MOS).

Language ROM Commands

SAVE "(afsp)", LOAD "(fsp)", CHAIN "(fsp)" are all accepted but not LOAD"". On a serial storage system such as tape, CHAIN "" would load and run the next available program. The disk system requires a definite filename. * transfers control to either the DFS or MOS or later to any other ROMPACK etc. that would accept the command. *(fsp) will load a program from the currently selected drive and depending on the condition of *OPT setting, would run the program once loaded. The run is however a function of the OPT command which means Option, and is described later.

MOS Commands

All MOS commands start with an asterisk (star) and should not be confused with normal Basic commands.

The commands start with the device, be it EPROM or ROM, which occupies the ROM socket at the right-hand side of the row of ROM sockets situated below the keyboard. If one of the devices recognizes the command, then the instruction is implemented, otherwise the command is passed around the system until it eventually is offered to the disk. In this way, machine code programs on the disk can be 'chained' using *(fsp), provided that *LIB has been set to indicate which drive and directory contains the programs, e.g. the Acorn *FORM40 *FORM80 programs work in this way. Acorn Computers Ltd. are the manufacturers of the BBC Microcomputer.

*SAVE "(fsp)"(START)(LENGTH)(RUN)
[*S.]

This command takes a section of memory specified by the start address(SSSS), and limited by the end address (EEEE) saving this section on the disk chosen in the file specification under a given filename. Usually *SAVE "(fsp)" is used to store machine code programs whilst SAVE "(fsp)" is used for Basic programs. The addresses and length values should be in hexadecimal and the '&' prefix, normal to the BBC Computer, is <u>not</u> required.

*SAVE "ACCOUNT" SSSS EEEE RRRR

or

*SAVE "ACCOUNT" SSSS+LLLL RRRR

If omitted the run (RRRR) address is assumed to be the same as the start address of the file, and the length of the file (LLLL) is calculated as the start address minus the end address + 1.

The address parameters of the SAVE command can be used to specify the number of bytes and thus create a file, albeit filled initially with rubbish, that can be used later within your program.

*SAVE "DATA" 00000 08000

Given the start address (00000) and the end address (07FFF) the file must be 128 sectors (32K). The data can be fed to the file later.

If you have a data file on a disk which contains other files you will reach a point where you cannot extend the data file to add new material (records) since one of the other files will be occupying the area into which you now wish to encroach. The saved area mentioned above does ensure that space is available for expansion.

The technique is often used with random access files to ensure that the length put aside is sufficient to allow for expansion of the files as new data is added.

*RUN (fsp)(parameters to Utility)
[*R.]

The specified machine code file is loaded into the computer and executed i.e. the same as CHAIN in Basic, the execution being from the run address given in the information saved or assumed previously (see *SAVE). To view the parameters applicable to the file use *INFO and *LIB.

The command will not run a Basic program. *(FSP) is accepted as being *RUN (fsp) and if the currently selected drive is being used then *(Filename) is also accepted as being *RUN(fsp).

*LOAD (fsp)(address)
[*L.]

Reads a machine code file from the disk into the memory placing it at the specified start address, or if such an address is not specified uses the file's own start address provided at the time of the *SAVE. The values given for addresses should be in Hex without an ampersand attached.

        *LOAD   WP   1900

The filename is accepted with or without quotation marks. The program can only be loaded from the currently selected directory and drive.

*SPOOL (fsp)
[*SP.]

This command is used to save a Basic program as it was entered from the keyboard, i.e. as a series of ASCII characters. Normally, when a Basic program is saved, the Basic keywords e.g. PRINT etc. are given a code value which only takes up a single memory location instead of several which would be necessary if all the characters of the keyword were stored. This method makes the program execute faster when run. A program stored in this way is called 'Tokenized'.

If a program is saved as ASCII characters it can be recovered later and added to other programs, provided that the line numbers do not coincide. If the line numbers do coincide with the program already in the computer, then that program will be overwritten by the incoming spool.

Using RENUMBER (Minimum abbreviation REN.), renumbers from 10 in increments of 10. If a different starting number and different increments are required they are specified in the command. For example, REN.100,5 causes renumbering from line 100 in increments of 5.

Assume a spool called "Dumper" is to be created with line numbers from 30000 which dumps the screen onto a printer. This program can be added to any existing program and treated as a procedure, called by 'PROCDump' when required.

The Dumper, let us imagine, has just been written and resides on line numbers 10 onwards. The requirement is to attach the dumper to a graphics program containing PROCDump at the appropriate place.

```
RENUMBER 30000
*SPOOL "DUMPER"        (opens the Text
                        File "Dumper)
LIST                    (output to screen
                        and to file)
*SPOOL                  (closes file Dumper
                        by affixing EOF
                        (End of File code)).

(BREAK)
NEW
LOAD "GRAPHIC"          (load in the Graphics
                        program)
REN.                    (renumber from
                        10 if required)
*EXEC "DUMPER"          (load in the spool)
RUN
```

If other routines are also required and are available as 'spools' all numbered at 30000 simply *EXEC the spool and renumber as required for each spool used. *BUILD and *SPOOL are ways of creating ASCII files.

*LIST (fsp)

Will display a 'Tokenized' listing onto the screen.
Files written with PRINT may also be listed with
this command.   These are the data files usually
taken out of an array within a program and stored
for re-use later under automatically generated
filenames (see 'WP').   Basic programs can be filed
in this 'token' fashion using *SPOOL.   *LIST is best
used in conjunction with 'page mode', which is
entered by CTRL/N.

*OPT (N)(n)

This command should not be confused with OPT to
be found in Basic.   Various effects can be achieved
according to the value of N and n.

*OPT
The default condition.

*OPT 1,0
disables the file information messages, e.g.
Load and execution addresses.

*OPT 1,n
enables the display of file information in the
same way as *INFO every time the file is
accessed, n must be greater than 0 and a space
or comma must exist between N and n.   n is
known as the argument of N.

When loading machine code tape files prior to
saving them onto the disk, you will need to know
where the computer will place them in memory,
how long the program is and where the run starts.

If you attempt to relocate the program into your
own addresses, any absolute jump values will be
invalid since they specify a definite address and relocation means that the address will no longer
contain the codes that it is meant to contain.

Only addresses which are relative remain valid after relocation.

*OPT 1,2
  will provide the detail you require as

        *TAPE
        *OPT 1,2
        *LOAD "(fsp)"

(fsp)(load address)(execution address)(length)

Full details of the *OPT settings are given in the User Guide on Page 398.

*OPT 2,n
  handles error detection during tape filing - see User Guide, Page 398.

*OPT 3,n
  sets the interblock gap used during recording - see User Guide, Page 398.

*OPT 4,(n)
  changes the auto-start of the currently selected drive. n can be 0,1,2 or 3 and all affect the course of action taken in response to the SHIFT and BREAK keys pressed together.

*OPT 4 0
  option off.

*OPT 4 1
  load a file called !BOOT.

*OPT 4 2
  Run a machine code file called !BOOT (not Basic).

*OPT 4 3
  EXEC a file called !BOOT.

Note the space between the command and (n). Without this space and for numbers greater than 4 an error message (&CB) bad option is produced.

!BOOT

The computer can be made to automatically load programs in response to the BREAK key being pressed. In most cases this response is arranged to occur only when the BREAK key is pressed whilst the SHIFT key is held down and the act is called BOOTING the system. !BOOT is pronounced pling boot.

!BOOT is a special filename. It is the name given to a file which can be 'built' directly onto the disk. The options, set by *OPT 4,(n) can act on this file in accordance with your choice of (n) with option 4 (The argument of OPT 4) e.g.

```
*OPT 4 3
*BUILD !BOOT          (create a BOOT file)
1 CHAIN "MENU"
2 (ESCAPE)            (terminate *BUILD)
```

The menu program called could be a list of programs contained on the disk and allows these programs to be called from the menu (see Chapter 5, Programming Problems and their Solutions).

The BOOT file should be in the default drive (0) and in directory ($), thus the fsp = 0:$.!BOOT

Since the BOOT is driven when BREAK is pressed with the SHIFT key held down (*OPT 4 3 set) the break causes a default to drive 0 and the directory defaults to $ (String). Thus the !BOOT file should be in the default drive (0) and stored in directory $ if it is to be an auto start file.

SWITCH OPTION

This feature can be fitted to 80 track drives to allow them to cope with 40 track disks. On some drives only a simple switch is required, on others a small electronic circuit. The effect is to create a double step pulse when moving from one track to the next. The system is made possible because the distance the drive read/write head moves on a 40 track drive corresponds to exactly two tracks on an 80 track drive.

	ERROR MESSAGES - Table 3.1	
&BD	Not enabled	(requires *ENABLE before the command)
&BE	Catalog full	(the Catalog can contain 31 files)
&BF	Can't extend	(not enough room for the increased file - Rename)
&C0	Too many open file	(only five allowed at once)
&C1	File read only	(you are trying to write to a locked file)
&C2	File open	(file is already open - you may require CLOSE # 0)
&C3	File locked	(you are trying to write to a protected file - see ACCESS)
&C4	File exists	(you are trying to rename using an existing filename)
&C5	Drive fault No @ track sector	(incorrectly formatted to suit your drive or mechanical fault)
&C6	Disk full	(try *COMPACT or replace disk - close files first)
&C7	Disk fault	(damaged disk, wrong format)
&C8	Disk changed	(the disk taken out has files still open)
&C9	Disk read only	(disk is write protected)
&CA	Bad sum	(check sum error - bad data or memory fault)
&CB	Bad option	(*OPT 1 or *OPT 4 (n) only, are allowed)
&CC	Bad filename	(Name longer than 7 letters etc.)
&CD	Bad drive	(: missing or drive number out of range 0-3)
&CE	Bad directory	(use only one letter directory name)
&CF	Bad attribute	(i.e. use only L with *ACCESS)
&D6	File not found	(are you on the right drive/disk/ Directory?)
&FE	Bad command	(* Omitted or command not recognized by DFS)

4 File Handling

File Handling in Basic

Programs and data can both be saved on a disk surface and are referred to as files.

Program Files

SAVE

Programs written in Basic are placed onto a disk using SAVE "(fsp)". It is not necessary to provide load or run addresses at the time of saving a program, since &FF1900 is assumed as the start address of Basic programs and &FF801F is assumed to be the execution address from which a program run commences. The filename used for disk purposes may have seven letters or numbers but must not use *:.!#or start with a number. Spaces within the name are not allowed, e.g.

    SAVE "TEST1"

The command saves all the memory which lies between the variables PAGE and TOP which, by definition, is the user program.

LOAD

Load is used to bring a Basic program from the disk into the computer's memory, starting at the address PAGE (&FF1900) on a BBC 'B' Computer fitted for disk handling. The user must type LOAD "(fsp)" to start the process. It is possible when using a cassette filing system to employ LOAD"", which is interpreted as 'Load the next file'. This is not usable on the disk system.

The new program, as it enters the memory, overwrites any program already in memory. All previously used variables are lost during the action other than A% to Z% and @% which are not changed.

Programs loaded into memory do not automatically run when the load is completed, this effect being often used when a LIST or editing is required. In many cases the ESCAPE key and BREAK key are conditioned such that, once a program is run, it is not possible to escape and still list the program. This is a poor show where computer literacy is concerned, but deemed necessary by the software vendors who expect financial returns for their effort.

Load cannot be used as part of a program line.

CHAIN

This command can be used in a program line, but not as a multi-statement line. The syntax is CHAIN "(fsp)" where the filename must be inside quotation marks. The filename must comply with that specified under LOAD, e.g.

CHAIN "$.TEST2"

Programs are loaded from the disk into memory at the address PAGE which is initially &FF1900. Once loaded the program will automatically execute. Since CHAIN can be part of a program, it is often used by one program to load and run another program. The effect on resident variables by this command is the same as that described under LOAD.

Data Files

OPENOUT

Openout is used to initialize a file intended to hold data. A channel number is allocated to a variable which is then used during all subsequent operations on that file. Any file which already exists bearing the same filename will be deleted unless it is access locked. A new file is created by the command which is initially without length, e.g.

F = OPENOUT ("TEST2")

Filesnames are described briefly under the heading SAVE.

Since the files on a disk can be limited in length by a second file placed near the end of the original file, it is best to create a file whose length is already established (see *SAVE). This can be done in Basic by creating a loop which places a number of records of known length into the original file, albeit initially filled with garbage. In the example below, assume that arrays have been previously dimensioned called A$(20), B$(20), N(20).

```
100  F=OPENOUT ("TEST2")
110  FOR R = 1 TO 20
120  PRINT#F,A$(R),N(R),B$(R)
130  NEXT R
140  CLOSE #F
```

The above program would create a file containing 20 records where each record consists of A$,N,B$. Note that after use the file is closed using CLOSE #F. Five files can be open at any one time, and to close more than one file, CLOSE #0 can be used.

PRINT # is used to actually save the information onto the file media, and is described more fully on the following pages.

OPENIN   (NOTE: Use OPENUP with new Basic)

Essentially this command opens a file for random access.   The information can be read into the computer memory, one byte, word or record at a time, then after the information has been updated it can be saved for further use, e.g.

```
10    DIM A$(20),B$(20),N(20)
20    F = OPENIN ("TEST2")
30    FOR R = 1 TO 20
40    INPUT#F, A$(R),N(R),B$(R)
50    NEXT R
60    CLOSE#F
```

Note that the order in which the items are recovered from the file has to be identical to the order in which they were saved. In this example A$,N,B$.   Again the file must be closed when it is no longer required, see OPENOUT.

It may well be the case that you do not require all the strings and numbers brought back into memory. In this event only one record is loaded, examined to see if it is the record you need and overwritten if not required by the next incoming record. A pointer (PTR) can be moved to indicate the position along the file reached by such repeated loading.

PRINT #

Used to store data in a file, usually in conjunction with OPENIN or OPENOUT commands. The format used where the data to be saved is a string, such as A$, is to save &00 XX $ where XX is a one byte number equal to the length of the string.   The string itself is saved backwards. This is known as 'internal format', e.g.

00 0B MAHTAL SIRI

Two types of numeric variables are available. These are Integer and Real variables. An Integer variable is a whole number between 2,147,483,648 and 2,147,483,647 and is stored in the computer occupying five bytes, i.e. &40 (tells the computer to expect an integer variable) followed by four bytes, least significant byte first. The binary number is stored as a 'twos complement' form which allows 31 bits to represent the actual size of number and the MSB represents the sign of the number. If the MSB is set for a negative number, then the 31 bits representing the size of the number are 'complemented', i.e. all 0's become 1's and vice versa, e.g.

(i)   +2 = 00000000 00000000 00000000 00000010
(&00000002)
MS byte   LS.Byte

(ii)   -2 = 11111111 11111111 11111111 11111110
(&FFFFFFFE)

To obtain the size of the negative number, the number is complemented (i.e. 1's become 0's etc.) and one added to the result.

i.e. Complement (ii) :-

00000000 00000000 00000000 00000001

= &00000001 = 1 (dec)

Add 1 to result:-

Answer = &00000002 = 2 (dec)

Real Variables are used when numbers greater than that possible with Integer Variables are required and also if decimal arithmetic is required. The computer can cope with numbers in the range $2x10^{38}$ and $2x10^{-38}$.

As real numbers can only be stored to 9 digit accuracy, a method called Scientific Notation is used. This converts the number to nine digits with eight decimal places multiplied by a power of ten, e.g.

$$543217654 = 5.43217654 \times 10^8$$

"mantissa" "exponent"

In the computer this number is stored in five bytes, the first byte being &FF followed by four bytes containing the mantissa (least significant bit first) with 31 bits representing the size and 1 bit representing the sign of the number, and finally, one byte containing the 'exponent'.

You can see from this that during a loading operation the computer is forewarned regarding the type of variable to expect by the first byte encountered. If this disagrees with the program's expectation, i.e. if the program is saying INPUT#F, A$ and the byte found is &40, then a type mismatch error is produced. Error trapping is therefore advisable to prevent the loss of the data should a loading error occur.

INPUT#

Information, be it numeric or strings is read from a disk into the computer's memory using this command. The assigned variables which hold the incoming data follow the command and are separated by commas. The data itself is in what is known as 'internal format' which is explained under the heading PRINT#. The file must be open before the command can be used using OPENIN, e.g.

    100 INPUT#F, A$,N,B$

New Basic requires OPENUP instead of OPENIN.

Programs constructed on machines fitted with New Basic using OPENIN will not run on an 'old' Basic machine.

BGET#, BPUT#

As their names imply these are used to Put or Get a single byte at a time from an open file. Since only one byte is involved the number must lie between &0 and &FF (0 to 255) otherwise 256 is subtracted repeatedly until the value is less than or equal to 255, e.g.

```
200    number = BGET#F
210    BPUT#F, number
```

PTR#

Pronounced 'Pointer hash', PTR# is used to select which item in a file, previously opened with OPENIN or OPENOUT, is to be handled next. The internal format described under the heading PRINT# is used within the file, thus an integer variable is 5 bytes long, real numbers 6 bytes, and strings occupy a length indicated by the second byte plus 2 bytes. When using PTR#, the file number or variable representing the file number is required after the hash symbol, e.g.

```
300    PRINT PTR#F, N%
310    PTR#F = PTR#F+25
320    REM reset the pointer to the start of
       the file
330    PTR#F=0
340    REM get record length for fixed length
       record file
350    INPUT#F,RL%
360    PTR#F = PTR#F+5
370    INPUT PTR#F,A$
380    PTR#F=PTR#F+RL%
390    REM now at start of next record
```

EXT#

Once a file has been opened using the OPENUP or
OPENOUT commands the total length of the file
can be obtained using EXT#(TEST2) the TEST2
being the (fsp) in these examples.

```
400    L=EXT#(TEST2)
410    PRINT L
```

Files can be extended by adding new records,
provided that the end of the file does not meet the
start of another file, saved on the same side of the
same disk. For this reason files are often created
with a known length using *SAVE.

EOF#

Every file created on the disk has at its end an end
of file marker (EOF). The function EOF# returns a
value 0 until the marker is reached, after which -1
is returned. When used the variable carrying the
channel number must also be employed, e.g.

```
420    REPEAT
430    PRINT#F,N%
440    UNTIL EOF#(F)
```

CLOSE#

Used to close a particular file or a group of open
files. On closing a file any data still in memory is
transferred to the media as required. CLOSE #0
closes all open files, e.g.

```
450    CLOSE #F
```

Although filing can be done in Basic it is to some
extent cumbersome. In the BBC Computer,
arrangements have been made for internal machine

code calls to handle the files for you. These are known collectively as the OSBYTE calls, although some of them handle considerably more than a byte as you will discover. The use of these calls is desirable since they do not interfere with the use of the TUBE, a device which allows the communication of dissimilar microprocessors. In any event, the OSBYTE calls can be looked upon by the user as internal subroutines which can be used for file handling.

When OPENOUT is used a file is created which is given a name and data is placed into that file. However, if a file already exists with that name it is overwritten by the new data. OPENUP allows the named file to be opened for random access without the whole file being overwritten. At present OPENUP is available written with 'new' Basic Roms, and OPENIN is used for random access in Basic programs.

Assembly Language File Handling

The BBC Computer operating system contains a series of subroutines arranged to handle files.

Table 5.1 shows the subroutines and their associated vectors, where vectors are memory locations holding the address (pointing to) the area of the operating system Read Only Memory (ROM) which contains the usable routine.

These indirection vectors consist of a 2 byte address which identifies the routine required. The address is stored with the lo-byte in the lower address and both locations are in the workspace memory area &0200 to &20FF. Code located in the paged ROMS can be called or calls to the paged ROMS can be intercepted using these vector locations.

Think of the vector location as a signpost telling you where to find an address.

Fig. 4.1 Vectors

Before we can properly understand the machine code facilities, it is necessary to discuss the 6502 microprocessor itself, this 'chip' (integrated circuit) being the heart of the BBC Microcomputer. We do not intend here to teach binary or hexadecimal notation, for many books are available at your local library covering these subjects. For the same reason, it is not intended to cover assembly language programming. Our intent here is concerned with the registers within the device handling blocks of memory.

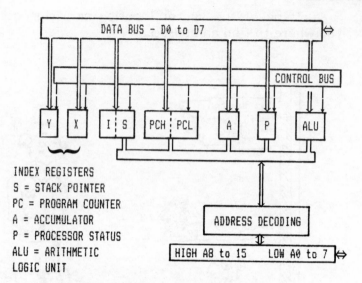

Fig. 4.2 Internal Structure of the 6502

Figure 4.2 represents a simplified view of the 6502 microprocessor. The chip has 16 address lines A0 to A15 and 8 lines which carry data, together with a number of control lines all of which link the device to the outside world.

Before arithmetic or logical operation takes place, the accumulator (A) usually contains one of the operands, and the other operand is usually in the memory location. The result of operation, be it logical or arithmetic, is placed in the accumulator. It may seem a little odd to work one area so hard and at the same time alter its original contents. After all, the original number may be required again! The original number in the accumulator usually was the result of a previous calculation and, if it is needed later, it can be stored in memory before the next operation is performed.

The main reason for the accumulator being the source and destination for the data is that it allows very short 'opcodes' (instructions) to be used, these being a single 'byte' (8 bits). If more than one 'register' were used to hold the information then more bits would be required to indicate which register contained the operand to be used in the next calculation. Although other microprocessors, e.g. Z80, 8080, sixteen-bit and thirty-two bit devices can handle the movement of large blocks of memory very efficiently, relatively simple commands often require three or four bytes in order for the commands to be executed, which entails a loss in execution speed. On the other hand the 6502 must always be loaded with the correct operand prior to use, which is sometimes inefficient.

It has been mentioned that the other operand is often in memory. The registers X and Y are used to point to the memory location containing the required data, and are often referred to as index registers for this reason.

All the registers (other than the program counter) within the 6502 handle 1 byte (8 bits) at a time, which gives the range of numbers as &00 to &FF per operation. Since the address of the various devices and memory require 16 bits (0 to 15 address lines) it is clear that indirect and indexed addressing methods have to be employed whenever memory management is involved. The various methods are outlined below in alphabetical order.

Absolute Addressing

Absolute addressing requires a 3-byte instruction. The first byte is interpreted as an instruction and the next two as the address in memory which either contains the data or into which the data should be placed when extracted from the accumulator, i.e.

STA &1234

requires the contents of the accumulator to be stored at the address Hex 1234.

There are more efficient ways of performing this task, as you will discover later. As you can see, the name 'absolute' is given since the full memory location is specified. The name 'extended addressing' is sometimes used for absolute addressing.

Direct Addressing (Zero Page)

If the memory location required lies in the area &00 to &FF then only one byte is required to convey the information. This means that an instruction (opcode) followed by the address byte will contain only two bytes instead of three for absolute address specification. The Machine Operating System utilizes quite a lot of these zero page locations and the functions employing this space can be seen in Table 4.3.

Zero page or direct addressing is also referred to as short addressing in contrast to absolute addressing. Only three machine cycles are employed and this mode, as well as offering a speed advantage and shorter codes, can be looked upon as being an extra register for the CPU (Central Processor Unit, i.e. 6502). The OSBYTE calls that we will be using later utilize zero page quite heavily.

Implied Addressing

Where opcodes operate on internal registers no addresses are required. The instruction implies the address by specifying the registers, i.e.

TAX = Transfer the contents of A to X

This type of instruction is usually encoded within 1 byte.

Immediate Addressing

Immediate addressing is the name given to instructions which load data into the registers at the same time as the opcode. This takes the form of an 8-bit data value following the opcode, e.g.

LDA#9

which means load the accumulator with the value 9.

Indexed Addressing

Indexed addressing is used when a block of memory, such as a table is to be accessed. It is achieved by the instruction specifying a register and an address where the contents of the register and the address are used in a combination that gives the final address required. The address part is usually zero page, thus a short address can be used to point to a value in zero page which contains a displacement

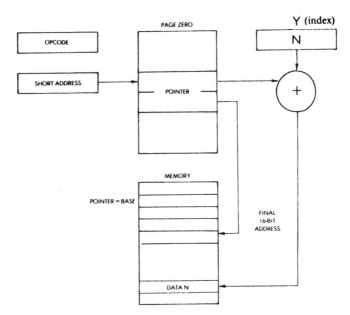

Fig. 4.3 Indexed Addressing

to a memory area whose start address is in a register, say X, thus giving rise to the final data address. There are two forms, pre-indexed and post-indexed.

In post-indexed addressing the final location is the sum of the contents of the index register plus a displacement word (2 bytes) obtained from the zero page address. It can be seen that post-indexed addressing uses two pointers - one 8-bit and one 16-bit to find the actual location within the block. The use of two pointers (both memory areas) without the internal register index is called indirect addressing, the locations being often referred to as vector locations.

In pre-indexed addressing (or indirect indexed addressing) the final location is obtained by accessing two zero page locations containing the final location address given by the sum of the 8-bit zero page base address given in the instructions and the contents of the Y index register.

The other types of indexed addressing are absolute indexed and zero page indexed.

An example of absolute indexed is the following instruction:

LDA TABLE, X

This means load the accumulator register with the contents of a memory location whose address is the sum of the 16-bit address allocated to TABLE and the 8-bit contents of the X register. Thus, TABLE in the base or starting address and subsequent location may be accessed by simply incrementing the X register.

Zero page indexed addressing is similar to absolute indexed addressing but in this case the final location is assumed to be in page zero of memory, therefore the base address is just 8 bits, giving a two byte instruction.

Relative Addressing

This form of addressing is usually used for jumping from one location to another which is specified as being relative to the first location. In other words the opcode is followed by an address byte then a second byte which is a displacement from the specified address, the displacement being limited to +128 or -127 locations, i.e.

BNE   &32   10

A table of relative displacements can be found at the end of this chapter. It is worth noting that a displacement of -1 is shown as &FF, 2 = &FE etc. The area that is being referred to by displacement values is $\pm X$ locations forward or backward from the location containing the instruction. This means that even if the program is moved into another block of memory the values are still true, whereas absolute address would need alteration.

Having mentioned zero page, it seems appropriate to say a little more about the 'page' system. Table 4.3 shows how the memory hibyte is used to indicate the page number where each page can contain 256 locations (&00 to &FF) low bytes (shown only in the zero page area).

TABLE 4.1 RELATIVE ADDRESS TABLES : FORWARD RELATIVE BRANCH

MSD\LSD	0	1	2	3	4	5	6	7	8	9	A	B	C	D	E	F
0	0	1	2	3	4	5	6	7	8	9	10	11	12	13	14	15
1	16	17	18	19	20	21	22	23	24	25	26	27	28	29	30	31
2	32	33	34	35	36	37	38	39	40	41	42	43	44	45	46	47
3	48	49	50	51	52	53	54	55	56	57	58	59	60	61	62	63
4	64	65	66	67	68	69	70	71	72	73	74	75	76	77	78	79
5	80	81	82	83	84	85	86	87	88	89	90	91	92	93	94	95
6	96	97	98	99	100	101	102	103	104	105	106	107	108	109	110	111
7	112	113	114	115	116	117	118	119	120	121	122	123	124	125	126	127

TABLE 4.2 RELATIVE ADDRESS TABLES : BACKWARD RELATIVE BRANCH

LSD MSD	0	1	2	3	4	5	6	7	8	9	A	B	C	D	E	F
8	128	127	126	125	124	123	122	121	120	119	118	117	116	115	114	113
9	112	111	110	109	108	107	106	105	104	103	102	101	100	99	98	97
A	96	95	94	93	92	91	90	89	88	87	86	85	84	83	82	81
B	80	79	78	77	76	75	74	73	72	71	70	69	68	67	66	65
C	64	63	62	61	60	59	58	57	56	55	54	53	52	51	50	49
D	48	47	46	45	44	43	42	41	40	39	38	37	36	35	34	33
E	32	31	30	29	28	27	26	25	24	23	22	21	20	19	18	17
F	16	15	14	13	12	11	10	9	8	7	6	5	4	3	2	1

TABLE 4.3 MEMORY USAGE O.S. 1.0 & GREATER

Page	Function
& 0000 & 0098 & 00B0 & 00B8 & 00D8 & 00E9	Zero page Language Zero page Operating system Zero page Econet Zero page Filing system Zero page VDU display Zero page Machine operating system
& 01 & 02 & 04 & 08 & 09 & 0A & 0B & 0C	Hardware stack descending downwards O.S. workspace (indirected) Language workspace O.S. workspace RS423 transmit buffer RS423 receive buffer Soft Key buffer Character definitions 128-255 (Not available if applications ROMS are fitted)
& 0D & 0E & 19	User machine code area User space on minimal model User space on disk model Screen memory 1K to 20K according to mode
& 80 & C0 & FC & FE & FF	Sideways ROMS O.S. ROM Reserved for future expansion Mapped input/output area O.S. calls See Table 5.1

5 Operating System Commands

Don't worry if you fail to fully understand the next few pages, the operating system will handle these matters for you. They are written only for the benefit of those who may require to interpret the operating system vectors.

At this point integer variables and indirection operators must be discussed.

INTEGER VARIABLES

When the power is first applied to the computer the integer variables A% to Z% are given values. Unlike other variables they are already assigned and the arrangement is to make A% to Z% = 0. The computer understands 0 to be equal to FALSE and -1 to be TRUE. The integers, once set, whatever their value, are not altered by chaining various programs into the computer and this means that parameters can be passed from program to program as integers.

Each integer occupies four successive bytes of memory and these can be made to hold the whole number portion of a number. If a number is offered which contains a fractional portion, then that portion is rounded up or the values after the decimal point are ignored.

The range within which an integer can lie is limited by the computer to between -2,147,483,648 and 2,147,483,647. Since operations with these numbers are considerably faster than with the normal 13-byte numeric variables they are often used in a program where speed is required sooner than accuracy, not that accuracy is lost to any great degree ($^{\pm}$.01 in 2,000,000).

The disk filing system will accept A% as accumulator, X% and Y% as X and Y registers and C% as the carry flag when operating system calls are made, providing that the conditions described in the commands which follow are met.

INDIRECTION OPERATORS

There are three operators available:

? Pronounced 'query', which affects one byte at a time.

! Pronounced 'pling!, known as a 'word' indirection operator and affects 4 bytes (the length of an integer variable).

$ Pronounced 'string', which affects from 1 - 256 bytes, 256 bytes being the maximum length of a string variable. The length of a string is known by its termination &0D (carriage return).

Using these operators we will be able to look at the contents of memory locations (PEEK) or place values into memory locations (POKE).

Assume that it is required to place 99 into location &3000, and that M is assigned as the variable containing the address.

M = &3000 : ?M = 99

To read the location and print the result would require

PRINT ?M

We could also say: X = ?M which would give X the value contained in the location (99) whereas X = M would make X = &3000.

From the above information it can be seen that M% could hold four bytes as   :   M% = &3000 : !M% = &89ABCDEF would arrange the memory as:

&3000   =   &EF
&3001   =   &CD
&3002   =   &AB
&3003   =   &89

PRINT~M% would give &3000 (~ = PRINT in Hex) and PRINT ~!M% would give &89ABCDEF since pling would involve the four locations each holding a byte. To prove this try PRINT ~ ?(M%+1) which can be written as ~M%?1

e.g.   ~ M%?3 = &89

Notice how the order is reversed and the numbers appear in memory as if read from right to left.

The string handling $M should not be confused with M$, for M$ = 'Whatever you want' placed wherever the computer decides to put it in memory. $M on the other hand is already set to a memory area at the beginning of possibly 256 bytes. The last byte to be entered into this block will be &0D (carriage return) and the start of the block would have been determined beforehand with M = &xxxx where xxxx is a memory location in RAM.

Computers fitted with operating systems capable of handling disks differ from the earlier versions in a number of ways, one of which is the re-allocation of memory as shown in Table 4.3.

The area required by the computer for use as workspace is increased and the figures derived from

*KEY0 DIM P%-1 : P. HIMEM-P% ¦M

Where the red user key 0 is thus defined to give the free
bytes for each mode:

1)	5,886	2)	5,886	3)	9,982
4)	16,126	5)	16,126	6)	18,174
7)	25,342				

At a glance it can be seen that many programs which
would run in a selected mode on a 'B' model can no longer
do so, due mainly to mismanagement of memory
allocation by the programmer. You can use these
programs by resetting the computer page to be the same
as its original (non-disk) value i.e.

```
PAGE = &E00
*TAPE
LOAD ""
```

An alternative method is to use what is known as an
offset loader to rearrange the locations, although in
many cases the matter is far more complicated than this.
In most cases the length of the program is at fault.

The user could extract all the text lines and create
a built file called by *TYPE (fsp) and thus save program
space, also re-assign the variables where possible to be
integers, not the 32-bit values that would be given to
non-integer variables.

Eliminate all REM statements, then change
multibyte descriptive variables to single, integer or
double character variables. In most cases that will do
the trick.

Passing Parameters

When the subroutine vectors are used via
indirection locations in page &02 the indirection
values require initialization. The 6502
microprocessor internal registers A, X and Y can
be used or zero page locations or a parameter block
in RAM or ROM.

The routines themselves are called using JSR to the appropriate location with the decimal flag CLEAR, i.e. the CPU (Central processor Unit) must be in binary mode before the call. On exit from the routine, D will be 0.

OSFIND

OSFIND opens a file for random access. Data can be read or written to the file and the file can be closed or terminated.

The value in the 'A' register on entry to the routine determines the type of operation performed and the options are as listed below.

> A=0   closes the specified files.
> A=64   opens a file for reading.
> A=128   opens a file for writing.
> A=192   opens a file for reading or writing (Random access)

If A is 128 (&80) or 192 (&C0) then the Y register must contain the high byte and the X register contains the low byte of an address which points to the filename in memory. On exit from the FIND routine, A contains the channel number used and this may be required later. In the program below, if Z% contains 0, then the operating system has been unable to open the file and this effect can be used to check for the existence of a file prior to creation of a file using OPENOUT.

The parameter for the Y register value is not passed back by the operating system to Y%. Should a value be required as a test for the existence of a file, the call should be made as follows, when the memory block has been set containing the filename and pointed to by X% and Y%:

```
OSFIND = & FFCE
Z% = USR(OSFIND)
Z% = Z% MOD 256
```

On return from the routine Z% will contain a value such as:

70 1C 37 11

Where the value 1C is Y% in this case, 37 is X% and the 11 is Z%. The last byte will be 0 if the file cannot be found.

If A=0 and Y=0 all files are closed including spool and exec files. If A is not zero, then A holds the number of files still open. The interrupt state is preserved and the flags are undefined (C, N, V and Z).

Close #0 can also be used to close all files.

OSFIND examples:

```
10      DIM M%30
20      I."ENTER FILENAME",F$ : REM USE
        TEST2 for F$
30      F$ = "$."+F$
40      PROCopen (&C0) : Open for random
        access
```

Line 10 sets aside a memory block into which the filename is to be placed as ASCII characters. These characters are then accessible using M?n or M!n, where n is a displacement from M.

At the time of 'booting' a menu program and selecting the program we wish to use, the menu places a particular directory onto the screen. Thus it is possible that a directory is selected to be in current use. For this reason any other filename we wish to access requires the full specification which includes the detail of the directory containing the file. We could set the library to assist with this point, but line 30 adds the correct directory to the entered filename to form the (fsp).

Should you prefer to enter the fsp for F$, then line 30 would not be required and the fsp would be easier to enter correctly if a catalog were shown on the screen, which could be arranged as

15 *.

Where such a directory is to be found on an alternative drive, then line 12 would be required.

12 *DRIVE(dr)

The whole lot can be placed together i.e.

30 F$ = ":(dr).(Dir)$."+F$

Since it is likely that 'Find' a file could be used in various places within the program, placing the actual find routine as a PROCEDURE allows this multiple usage. The type of purpose the file is opened for is carried as the parameter in brackets and passed to A%, which will later be given to the accumulator by the operating system.

To continue, assume the procedure 'Open' (note the lower case name, which avoids confusing the interpreter) lies at line number 2000.

```
2000   DEFPROCopen (4%)
2010 $M%=F$
```

We have now given the block M% the values for the (fsp) previously constructed. To see this in action, try

```
  50   END
2020   FOR R=0 to 7
2030   PRINT M%+R;"      ",M%?R;"      ",CHR$
       ((M%)R)
2040   NEXT
2050   ENDPROC
```

When run this will print out the memory address in hex followed by the ASCII code that the address contains followed by the character string that the code represents as:

1992	24	$
1993	2E	.
1994	54	T
1995	45	E
1996	53	S
1997	54	T
1998	32	2
1999	D	

Notice that the start of the block is where R=0 (M0), not M1, that the characters are stored the right way round, and that the string is terminated with &0D (carriage return).

To point X and Y to the address required we can give X% and Y% the values that are required, with Y% given the high byte, as in

    2020   Y%=M%DIV 256
    2030   X%=M%MOD 256

To test this now try a RUN with

    2040   PRINT "Y%="; ~Y%;"X%="; ~X%

and you will see the address contained.

All that remains is to zero C% to reset the carry flag; then we are able to call the operating system routine to find the file:

    2040   C%=0
    2050   Z%=(USR &FFCE)
    2060   Z%=Z% MOD 256
    2070   ENDPROC

Having opened a file by name, Z% contains what is known as the file 'handle' (for channel number). Handle is a CB (Citizens Band radio) term. In the context of this book Z% holds a number between 1 and 255, where this number is the channel number allocated to the file.

A 'PROCEDURE' is similar to GOSUB except that where RETURN would be used to pass the program back to the line after the call, ENDPROC is used instead. With a GOSUB a line number is given which is the start of the subroutine whilst PROCEDURE does not require a line number to be specified.

OSARGS

Having opened a file, OSARGS (&FFDA called via &0214) can be used to read and write the attributes of the file. To do this X must point to 4 locations in the zero page. Y contains the file handle and A specifies the type of operation. Z% will hold the handle assigned. Assuming the zero page locations to be &80 to &83 then Y% = Z% and X% = &80.

A = 0   reads the sequential pointer

A = 1   writes the sequential pointer

A = 2   reads the length of the file (EXTENT)

A = 255 means 'Ensure the file is up to date on the media'.

These results will be retained only if Y is not 0.

If Y is 0 then the value of A sets the required operation.

If A = 0 the type of filing system in use will be returned in A where the value for A is listed below.

A = 16   will return the address of the
          command line at X
A = 255   will ensure that all open files
          are up to date on the media

0   no file
1   1200 baud tape
2   300 baud tape
3   ROM pack
4   disk
5   Econet
6   Teletext/Prestel 'Telesoft'

The four locations in zero page should lie between 70 and 8F, which has been allocated for user routines.

The pointer can be moved along the file to access particular blocks where the block length is known. This pointer in effect moves sequentially along the length of a file and can be considered as an index marker. At the beginning of a file the pointer is set to 0.

OSFILE

Files are treated as sequences of 8-bit bytes which can be accessed by OSFILE in one operation. The routine is entered at &FFDD indirected by &212.

The X and Y registers must point to an 18 byte block of memory with X containing the low byte. This block is then arranged as follows:

0   address of file name (where the
      name is terminated by &0D).
2   load address 4 bytes (2 = LSB)
6   run address
&0A   start address of data for write operations
      of length of file for read purposes
&0E   end address of data (4 bytes with
      &0E as LSB).

The response for the value of A are

A = 0   save section of memory as a file (catalog information is also written)
A = 1   write the catalog information
A = 2   write the load address
A = 3   write the run address
A = 4   write the attributes
A = 5   read the file's catalog
A = 6   delete the file
A = 255   read the file's catalog information and load the file.

OSGBPB

Gets a byte block or puts a byte block. The call address is &FFD1 via &021A. The instruction block containing the detail of the type of operation required is pointed to by X and Y with X holding the low byte.

A = 1   means put byte using offset
A = 2   means put byte (no offset)
A = 3   means get byte using offset
A = 4   means get byte (no offset)

The offset values determine the type of operation, where

0   handle (channel number)
1   pointer to data
5   number of bytes to transfer
9 to D   bytes offset in file.

On exit if C = 0, then the transfer was successful. The bytes offset would be modified to indicate how much data has been transferred and gives rise to a new pointer value which is the old pointer plus the amount of data transferred. For example,

amend line 10 in our test program to read:

10   DIM M%30,X%20,

Note that X% is now already set to a memory block. Y% can be set as Y% = X% DIV 256 and values can now be assigned as X%!1=M% : A% = 5 : CALL OSGBPB

For further examples of the use of OSGBPB see the disk menu program.

OSBPUT

FFD4 via &218 will write a byte in A to an open file. Y contains the channel number on entry which is the result of OSFIND.

The pointer, set by OSARGS, shows the position in the file where OSBPUT or OSBGET is actioned.

OSBGET

FFD7 via &216 fetches a byte from an open file into A, the channel number being in Y as the result of OSFIND. On exit if C=0 the character in A is valid, otherwise A carries the error code. If A = &FE, then the end of file is indicated. The user should be aware of the reverse order that stored information utilizes.

OSWORD

Call FFF1 via 020C with A set to &7F enables you to read or write diskette sectors. X and Y point to a data block which is set as follows:

Offset	Function
0	drive number
1-4	start address data source or destination
5	number of parameters
6	command
7	parameters
etc.	parameters.

e.g. with the number of parameters as 3 the command can be &53 to read or &4B to write.

Parameter
1   track number
2   sector number
3   &21 (=one 256 byte sector)

On exit 0 will be placed at the end of the data block for a valid operation, otherwise the fault number will be placed at the same location.

If the OSWORD is not recognized by the operating system ROM it will be offered to the other ROMS present. For other OSWORD actions, see the BBC Computer User Guide Pages 458-463.

OSCLI

Call FFF7 via &0208. The command line interpreter can be accessed simply by placing an asterisk in front of the command, i.e.

*DISK

The call is thus more often used by machine language programs than high level languages. If X and Y point to the line to be interpreted it should not start with an asterisk, and the command line must end of &0D.

*DRIVE 1

is equal to:

```
10   DIM V 20
20   $V="DRIVE 1"
30   X%=V MOD 256
40   Y%=V DIV 256
50   CALL &FFF7
```

Table 5.1 shows a list of internal subroutines known collectively as the OSBYTE calls even though a few of them operate on considerably more than a byte.

TABLE 5.1 INTERNAL SUBROUTINES AND VECTORS

Name	Address	Vector	Address	Function
OSFIND	&FFCE	FINDV	&021C	Opens a file for update
OSARGS	&FFDA	ARGSV	&0214	Handles a file's attribute
OSFILE	&FFDD	FileV	&0212	Handles the data and catalog
OSGBPB	FFD1	GBPB	&021A	Reads/writes bytes to a file
OSBGET	&FFD7	BGETV	&0216	Reads a byte
OSBPUT	&FFD4	BPUTV	&0218	Writes a byte
OSWORD	&FFF1	WORDV	&020C	See list of effects in the User Manual
OSCLI	&FFF7	CLIV	&0208	Passes a command to the interpreter

RANDOM FILES

What follows is a brief description intended to familiarize the reader with certain terms which could be met in the ensuing chapters. The commands below are more fully explained under the heading Basic File Handling.

Random Access File is the name given to a file constructed in such a way as to allow rapid searches to take place. The head can be moved to any specific place within the length of the file being guided by a pointer (PTR#). The computer is aware of the length of the file (EXT # = extent) and can freely read from and write to the file. Reading and writing with the file is very fast, due to the fact that it is not necessary to read the whole file as you would have to do on a cassette tape or other serial device. The pointer allows the search or sort to take place within a few blocks.

The end of the file is marked with and end-of-file signal (EOF #); this contains a value of -1 (true) when the end has been reached or 0 (false) otherwise.

To start a file use X = OPENOUT (Filename) (note the brackets) or to open the file to read or write, use X = OPENIN (filename), or X = OPENUP.

Whe using OPENOUT, if a file already exists by that name then it is deleted unless checks and error trapping are taken care of. When a random file is created 64 sectors (1 sector = 256 bytes) or the length of an existing file by that name is reserved in RAM. If insufficient space exists, then an error message is produced. Initially PTR# and EXT# are both set to 0. The first 256 bytes of the file are loaded in RAM and this memory is known as the 'buffer'. After closing the file, the sector is re-stored on disk. When OPENOUT is called the file name is deleted and the buffer loaded.

Careful study of the programs will clarify the idea.

Usually the data is placed into pre-defined slots of known length and the file is divided out beforehand by giving dummy strings or by incrementing the pointer to the next block position. (Fig. 5.1)

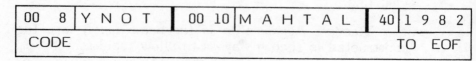

00	8	Y	N	O	T		00	10	M	A	H	T	A	L		40	1	9	8	2
CODE																		TO	EOF	

Fig. 5.1 File Arrangement

The strings are saved in the file backwards and each is preceded by a code &00 (Hex 0) + n to signify that a string follows, plus a digit showing the length of the block. The &40 tells the computer that an integer follows and the number is given in the next four bytes. Since integers are of fixed length no second code for length is required. &FF means that a real number follows, and the number then occupies the next 5 bytes. The number is stored in exponential format i.e.

$$1E-3 = 0.001$$

You can see from this that if you read within a loop a set of 'blocks' and the loop is asking for two strings plus a number, then if the data were presented differently an error would be produced (type mismatch).

6 File Program Examples

Records

The records that you may require on file usually consist of related items where the whole of the items are required to give the information true meaning, e.g.

Name, address, postcode, telephone number

Usually one of these items is used to locate the others and this is called a KEY FIELD, i.e. the name. A key field is usually the one sought by the search operations in order that the other items may be modified. Sometimes it is necessary to access records by different key fields according to the program requirements in charge of the data.

The term SORTING is used throughout this book when describing data being placed in some particular order i.e. alphabetically or similar sequence.

The term SEARCHING refers to the act of finding a record or key field in order to locate the related items.

85

A FIELD is the name used to describe the items stored within a Record.

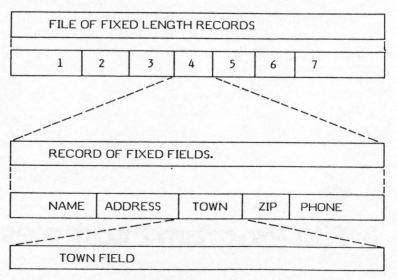

Fig. 6.1 Records and Fields

Consider trying to create a program which serves as a menu for any disk it happens to be placed onto. The advantage of this is that we could copy the menu onto the new disk then carry on writing our database, accounts package or whatever. We could of course create the menu directly onto a BUILT !BOOT file and set the OPTION to run this program, but the difficulty would be in editing any errors, or changing values to suit the requirements of the new disk. What we do is build a simple BOOT file as follows:

```
*TITLE "DISK NAME"
*OPT 4 3
*BUILD !BOOT
 1 CHAIN "MENU"
 2 (ESCAPE)
```

The problem now of course is, was our computer in a situation where the directory was thought to be other than $? If we are to create a menu then it has to list only a specified directory and not all the support files that may be present on the same disk.

Not so! This problem of having to write the complete (fsp) on a program requires your awareness but does not arise on a BOOT file since the file is initiated by the BREAK key and SHIFT key together. As you know, the BREAK key returns the directory to $ automatically. However, when you reach the point where a newly written 'Menu' program needs to be saved, ensure that you place it in DIR $.

Now let us consider the disk menu program which serves as an example of reading parameter from the disk, into memory.

```
10   REM **DISK MENU PROGRAM***
12   REM COPYRIGHT (C) TONY LATHAM 1982
14   REM THE COMPUTER USERS CLUB
20   MODE7
```

Now we can have 31 files on a disk so we must dimension an array to hold their names and put aside memory for the 'info' details.

```
40   DIM S%30,T%(31),X%20,File$(31)
50   F%=0
90   Y%=X% DIV 256
100  OSGBPB = &FFD1
110  Oscli = &FFF7
120  X%!1=S%
130  A%=5
140  CALL OSGBPB
150  I%=S%?0+1
160  REPEAT
170  I%=I%-1
180  UNTIL S%?I%<>0
185  S%?(I%+1)=13
190  REM ***PRINT HEADING***
200  Head$=$(S%+1)
210  PROCHead
220  PRINT'
```

In line 100, OSGBPB is the subroutine (courtesy of the operating system) which enables a block of bytes to be fetched or saved from a disk file which has already been opened by OSFIND. The &FFD1 opens the routine which vectors via &21A. In effect a complete block of memory can be loaded or saved. The X and Y registers of the 6502 need to be set to the area of memory to be used, with X given the low byte and Y the high byte.

Oscli in line 110 refers to operating system command line interpreter which vectors via &208. In other words the memory address &208 (& means hexadecimal number follows) contains the address of the routine to be used.

The block of memory S%(X) is loaded with bytes called from the disk by OSGBPB. S%+1 holds the values whose ASCII meanings will write the TITLE assigned to the disk (later to become Head$). This value is passed to the procedure within brackets. P.' means PRINT:PRINT.

The program continues:

```
380  X%!9=0
390  *DIR X
400  T%=0 : I%=0
410  X%!1=S%
420  X%!5=1
430  A%=8
440  E%=(USR OSGBPB) AND &1000000
450  IF E% <>0 AND T% = -1 THEN 590
460  IF E%=0 THEN 520
470  REM ** SET DIRECTORY **
480  *DIR A
490  T%=-1
500  X%!9=0
510  GOTO 410
520  S%?(S%?0+1)=13
530  File$(I%)=$(S%+1)
540  T%(I%)=T%
```

```
550   IF F%=0 THEN VDU 130,(I%+65);:PRINT
      TAB (4);File$(I%);TAB(19);:F%=1 : GOTO 570
560   IF F%>0 THEN VDU 130,(I%+65);: PRINT
      TAB (23);File$(I%):F%=0
570   I%=I%+1
580   GOTO 410
```

What we are doing is fetching the filenames of any files stored in DIR A (specified at line 480) and printing them onto the screen in two columns (TAB(4) and TAB(23)). If E% AND T% are both TRUE the action is stopped. I% is used as an 'index' pointer which is incremented at line 570 until all the filenames contained in that directory have been loaded into memory.

F% is used as a toggle to place the filenames first into one column then into the other, being set and reset in lines 550 and 560. The same two lines assign an alphabetic letter to each filename which will be the key to press in order that the program fixed by that letter should be chained.

```
590   VDU 26; 31,0,23;
600   PROCCol
610   PRINT C$; TAB(7,23); "ENTER PROGRAM
      LETTER?";
620   G%=GET
630   G%=G%-65
640   IF G% <0 OR G%>I% THEN PRINT "TRY
      AGAIN"; : GOTO 610
650   D%=0
655   CLS
660   IF T%(G%).<> 0 THEN CHAIN "A." +
      File$(G%)
670   $X%="RUN X."+File$(G%)
680   CALL Oscli
690   END
```

When a valid program letter is entered the associated file is CHAINED unless it is a machine code program. The latter is run by line 670. CALL Oscli executes the command line, which is seen to be either line 660 or 670 according to the type of program present.

```
700   DEFPROCHead
710   PROCCol
720   TB=(40-LEN(Head$))/2
730   PRINT C$;CHR$141; TAB(TB);Head$
740   PRINT C$;CHR$141; TAB(TB);Head$
750   ENDPROC
```

Lines 700 to 750 print the DISK TITLE in double height
characters into the centre of a background block at the
top of the screen.   The block itself is given a random
color.

Line 720 centers the text by fixing the TAB value.

```
760   DEFPROCCol
770   Back = RND(6)+129
780   Front = Back-1
790   Back$=CHR$(Back)+CHR$157
800   Front$=CHR$(Front)
810   C$=Back$+Front$
820   ENDPROC
```

The above serve to show the power and ability of the
operating system calls. However you may from time to
time require simply to save an array.   The following
program is an extract from a word-processing program
issued by the Computer Users Club in April 1982.

Although the listing of the full program is given
there are better ways of handling text once you have a
disk system. However, the file handling of the array
either to tape or disk will serve as a fine example.

The array consist of 61 strings T$(61) the length of
which has been pre-set to a value, typically 65
characters.   As each line is entered it is stored in the
array and a line pointer L% incremented.   Various
commands, embedded in the lines of text are recognized
and used to invoke printer changes etc. The user key f1
calls tape handling and f9 calls disk files. We will start
at the point where f9 has been pressed and the
proceedings directed to disk handling.

```
2120 *DISK
2130 INPUT "WHICH DRIVE FOR DATA",G%
2140 IF G% = 3 THEN *DRIVE 3
2150 IF G% = 2 THEN *DRIVE 2
2160 IF G% = 1 THEN *DRIVE 1
2165 IF G% = 0 THEN *DRIVE 0
2170 *DIR $
2180 T$(L%)=""REM CANCEL DISK CALL SIGNAL
2190 F%=1
2200 GOTO 910
```

All is straightforward so far - we have changed filing system from TAPE to DISK and selected a drive, then ensured that the directory for the text file is $ (which would not show on the menu). Line 910 is one line further on to where tape handling would start so I will also show line 900.

```
900  *TAPE
910  INPUT    TAB(7),"DO    YOU    WISH    TO
     LOAD",QU$
920  IF LEFT$(QU$,1)="Y" THEN PROCFETCH :
     GOTO 250
930  PROCDITCH : GOTO 250
```

This small section arranges for the files to be either incoming or outgoing and after the relevant procedure has been executed returns to awaiting keyboard inputs at line 250.

```
1350 DEFPROCFETCH
1360 IF F% >0 THEN F%=0 : *.
```

If the flag F% is set then before getting a file from the disk the directory of filenames is presented. The line 1360 in conjunction with 2190 is used to set the flag as required.

```
1380 INPUT   "DO   YOU   WANT   A   SPECIAL
     FILE",DU$
1390 IF DU$="YES" OR DU$ = "Y" THEN
             PROCCHANGE : GOTO 1420
1400 INPUT "WHICH PAGE NUMBER", QU%
1410 A$ = "PAGE"+STR$(QU%)
```

The filename is created by the word page + a number unless you specify otherwise. The arrangement allows you to create a book with each page being saved under a name which is numerically incremented.

```
1420 ON ERROR GOTO 1520
1430 B=OPENIN (A$)
1440 L%=1
1450 REPEAT
1460 INPUT # B,T$(L%)
1470 L%=L%+1
1480 UNTIL EOF#B
1490 CLOSE # B
1500 L%=L%-1
1510 ENDPROC
```

At line 1430 the computer opens a channel by assigning a channel number - in this case to 'B', the REPEAT UNTIL LOOP (Lines 1450 to 1480) fetches the file into the array, one line at a time until the EOF (end of file) signal is seen, after which the file is closed.

```
1520 REPORT
1530 P. "SORRY-ERROR"
1540 IF ERR=17 THEN END
```

The above few lines form error trapping. Error 17 is the escape key and is allowed to end the program.

```
1560 DEFPROCDITCH
1570 A$="PAGE"+STR$(C%)
1580 PRINT "THIS FILENAME IS"
1590 PRINT
1600 PRINT TAB(6),A$
1610 PRINT
1620 INPUT "DO YOU WISH TO CHANGE THIS",
     QU$
1630 A$="PAGE"+STR$(C%)
1640 IF LEFT$(QU$,1)="Y" THEN PROCCHANGE
1650 PRINT "INSERT DATA DISK (TAPE SET FOR
     RECORD)"
1660 INPUT "ENTER WHEN READY",G%
1670 ON ERROR GOTO 1770
1680 B=OPENOUT(A$)
```

```
1690 FOR R=1 TO L%
1700 PRINT # B,T$(R)
1710 NEXT R
1720 CLOSE #B
1730 C%=C%+1
1735 IF F%=0 THEN 1750
1740 *.
1750 INPUT "KEY=CONTINUE" G%
1760 ENDPROC
```

Again the filename is constructed from the word PAGE plus a number less otherwise specififed. After the array is saved by the loop 1690 to 1710 the file is closed and the updated catalog is displayed at line 1740. The wait at 1750 allows the user to read the catalog then enter a key to return to the entry of commands or text. PROCCHANGE, referred to in line 1640 allows the user to construct an alternative filename.

```
1810 DEFPROCCHANGE
1820 INPUT "WHAT NAME",D$
1830 INPUT "WHAT NUMBER",C%
1840 A$=D$+STR$(C%)
1850 ENDPROC
```

The trouble with loading files of any length for updating lines with the amount of available memory after the screen and the program space is deducted. Large arrays use considerable amounts of memory, for example 60 lines of 65 characters uses 6900 bytes if the screen is in 80 character mode (Mode 0 or 3), and the screen uses 20K.

Total memory then becomes 26,900 leaving approximately 7K of available space for the program. One way of ensuring that all available space is used is to calculate the memory left and use that space to enter the array dimension.

```
B%=HIMEM-LOMEM-2000   :   S%=(B%/256):DIM
T$(S%)
```

The -2000 allows for 1600 of RAM used at the start of program area plus 400 bytes for other variables.

Random Access Examples

In the examples which follow, files of any length containing data may be created and data in these files may be accessed regardless of where it may be within the file. The ability to read and write to any part of a disk file forms the basis of Database Management Systems.

Two programs are listed which are used to demonstrate how, by using the operating system routines OSFILE, OSFIND, OSARGS and OSGBPB and supplying the necessary parameters e.g. load and data addresses, you can read and write bytes direct to a file you have created using the first program.

The first program uses the operating system routine OSFILE to create a new file by specifying it's name, load and execution addresses and data start and end addresses.

Details of the OSFILE routine can be found in the User Guide p. 454-456 and it can be seen that OSFILE can perform 8 different operations set by a value sent to the A register with parameters being held in a control block. The program prompts you to supply a filename and then asks you to specify the operation you want by inputting a value for A.

The program then asks you to supply parameters for the operation you have selected. Assuming that you want to save a section of memory (A=0) which is the way in which you may create a dummy file for data of any length you like which is not limited by the amount of available computer memory. The maximum length is only limited by how much space you have available on the disk, e.g. a data file might need to be 64K! For this operation you need to supply the file load address, execution address, start and end data addresses. When deciding on the load address required, this would need to be clear of the Basic program and variables.

By printing the value of TOP, you can see where Basic ends. In the case of the second program - the file processor, a convenient address can be 9000 decimal. The execution address can be set to be the same as the load address which is normally the case with machine code programs. If the file contains data then the execution address is irrelevant and can be again set to the load address. With files containing Basic the load address is normally &FFFF 1900 and the execution address &FFFF 801F. The last two parameters are the data start and end addresses.

The start address would normally point to the start in memory of the data, Basic, machine code etc. If the file contains data, the start address can be set to the lowest available spare location as with the load and execution addresses.

The data end address is the important address from which the file length is calculated. As all the addresses can be specified as 32-bit, then the maximum end address is &FFFF FFFF which is 4,294,967,296(dec) which is for all intents and purposes limitless!

When creating a file of say 64K there is no need to worry about the fact that the end address is outside the range of the computer's memory as once the highest memory location has been read, writing will start again at location 0 and will continue until the required number of bytes have been transferred. This operation must be carried out to reserve the total space on the disk as it is not possible to extend the file if all the data space has been taken up.

This is because if there was another file following this data file then to extend the data file would mean overwriting the following file. If however, there was no following file the data file would be extended but this condition cannot always be guaranteed and it is safer to estimate the total length and reserve space on the disk.

Once you have created this file it will of course contain a certain amount of rubbish and therefore the next step would be to initialize the bytes within the file i.e. set the bytes to &00 say.

This would involve using the process contained in the second program to write blocks of &00 of convenient size set up in memory as a series of write operations to fill up the entire file.

Going back to the OSFILE program, when the write operation has been performed the 'control block' is updated by overwriting the data start and end addresses with the file length and file attributes respectively, which can be saved and used later.

This covers the writing of a new file and the rest of the OSFILE operations concern loading a specified file (A=&FF) which would load the file into memory and store the catalogue information, i.e. load, execution addresses, length etc. in the control block.

The demonstration program will list out the contents of the control block which you can compare with the information produced when typing *INFO(afsp). Other operations enable you to alter load, execution and attributes values by setting the new address or attributes in the control block and performing the OSFILE operation. This will cause the catalog information on the disk to be altered but these are the only changes you can make to an existing file. If you want to alter the file length then the file must be re-written completely as a new file.

The final operation is to delete a file (A=6). In this case only the filename need be input.

One word of warning concerning loading files using OSFILE. The computer will try and load the entire file and if this happens to be a data file of large size, e.g. 64K, then there will come a point where vital operating system locations will be overwritten resulting in very odd patterns appearing on the screen and finally causing the picture on the screen to break up completely.

Recovery can be done by pressing BREAK but all programs and data will be lost. However, if this is done accidentally then the file and disk will not be corrupted. Therefore before doing any loading operations make sure that your current program has been saved on disk beforehand.

OSFILE Program Notes

Lines 70-90 input the filename and stores it in a series of locations starting at &0DB0 using the $ indirection operator, see User Guide p.409.

Lines 120-250 input information required for OSFILE and also set the control block to hold this information in locations &0DB0-&0D91. The filename and control block addresses were chosen so that the contents would not be overwritten when loading data or programs and use the area &0D80-&0DFF which have been set aside for the user.

Note that locations &0D00-&0D7F are required for use by the disk and Econet routines.

Lines 270-350 contain the assembly code to set the A register for the operation required and X, Y registers to the start of the control block. After OSFILE is called then the A register contains the 'file type' which is saved in &0D9F.

Lines 380-430 are used to output the file type and the contents of the control block, &0D9F and &0D82-&0D91 respectively.

```
>L.
  10 REM DEMO FOR LOAD/SAVE FILES USING OSFILE
  20 REM M.Sein - Computer Users Club
  30 MODE 7
  40 DIM MEM 100
  50 P%=MEM
  60 PRINT'"XXFILE READ/WRITE DEMO - OSFILEXX":PRINT
  70 INPUT"Filename?"F$
  80 F%=&0DB0
  90 $F%=F$
 100 !&0D80=F%
 110 OSFILE=&FFDD
 120 REM XXSET UP CONTROL BLOCK AT &0D80
 130 INPUT"OPERATION REQD(A=?) "OP
 140 IF OP=2 INPUT"REQD LOAD ADDR(dec) "TRANS%:!&0D82=TRANS%:GOTO 260
 150 IF OP=3 INPUT"REQD EXEC ADDR(dec) "EXEC%:!&0D86=EXEC%:GOTO 260
 160 IF OP=4 INPUT"REQD ATTRIBUTES(dec) "DEN%:!&0D8E=DEN%:GOTO 260
 170 IF OP=6 OR OP=5THEN 260
 180 INPUT"REQD LOAD ADDR(dec) "TRANS%
 190 INPUT"REQD EXEC ADDR(dec) "EXEC%
 200 INPUT"REQD DATA START ADDR(dec) "DAT%
 210 INPUT"DATA END ADDR(dec) "DEN%
 220 !&0D82=TRANS%
 230 !&0D86=EXEC%
 240 !&0D8A=DAT%
 250 !&0D8E=DEN%
 260 REM XXSETUP OSFILE
 270 [OPT0
 280 .INIT
 290 LDA £OP\Function reqd
 300 LDX #&80\Set Ctrl Blk lo byte
 310 LDY #&0D\Set Ctrl Blk hi byte
 320 JSR OSFILE
 330 STA &0D9F\Save File Type
 340 RTS
 350 ]
 360 CALL INIT
 370 IF OP=1 OR OP=2 OR OP=3 OR OP=4 OR OP=6 THEN 440
 380 PRINT'"XXINFO RETURNED IN CTRL BLKXX"
 390 PRINT"FILE TYPE(hex) ";~?&0D9F
 400 PRINT"LOAD ADDR(hex) ";~!&0D82
 410 PRINT"EXEC ADDR(hex) ";~!&0D86
 420 PRINT"LENGTH OF FILE(hex) ";~!&0D8A
 430 PRINT"FILE ATTRIBUTES(hex) ";~!&0D8E
 440 REM
 450 END
```

File Processing

This section involves the use of OSFIND, OSGBPB and OSARGS and how they are used to read and write bytes to a selected file.

The OSFIND routine is described on page 451 of the User Guide and is used to open a file for reading or writing by allocating a 'channel' number which the computer uses as a reference for future access operations. Several files may be opened simultaneously and each has a channel allocated to it, and this number is always used by the operating system routines to know which file is to be handled. The demonstration program asks you for the filename of the data file you have created using the first program and then calls OSFILE to open the file for input and output (Random Access), this operation is selected by setting the A register to &C0. Other values of A can open a file just for reading or just for writing but for data handling you would normally be reading from and up-dating the data as well, therefore random access would normally be selected. The remaining operation is to close the file (A=0) which will close specific files by specifying the channel number or close all opened files if channel 0 is specified.

Closing files when finished with should be done to enable the channel to be cleared for another file if needed, as there are only a limited number of channels available. The demonstration program will, after a channel has been assigned, output the channel number and this will be found to be &11 if only one file has been opened. If however the filename is not found then the channel number (returned in the A register) will be &00 and the program outputs the message 'File not found'.

The file required for operation is now opened and the next procedure is to actually access the information. The OSGBPB routine is used and this forms the heart of the process of writing and reading to any section of the file. This routine again can perform various operations depending on a value sent to the A register.

These are:

A=&01   - Write byte using a byte offset
A=&02   - Write byte ignoring byte offset
A=&03   - Read byte using a byte offset
A=&04   - Read byte ignoring byte offset

The most important aspect of the file handling is this 'byte offset'. This offset is in fact a sequential pointer which represents an index (counting the beginning of the file as zero) of the next byte on the file to be accessed. Thus if this pointer were set to, say 100, and a read operation was required, then the first 100 bytes on the file would be ignored and the 100th byte would be the first one to be transferred to memory. Similarly, if a write operation was required then the first 100 bytes on the file would be left.

Thus for data handling, reading and writing would be done by selecting just A=&03 or A=&01 respectively. The other information required by OSGBPB is the file channel number (derived using OSFIND), the number of bytes to be read or written, and the data pointer which is a 32-bit address pointer specifies where in the computer's memory data is to be 'saved' from or where data from the file is to be loaded to. The demonstration program will request all this information which will be set up as a 'control block' in memory addresses &0D80-&0D8C consisting of:

i)   Channel No. (or handle) - 1 byte

ii)   Data Pointer (4 bytes - LSB first)

iii)   No. of bytes to transfer (4 bytes - LSB first)

iv)   Byte Offset (4 bytes - LSB first)

Similar to the OSFILE routine, results are returned to the control block and these affect the data and byte offset pointers.

The data pointer is up-dated to point to the next location in memory following the last byte to be transferred i.e. if the start address was 9000 and 100 bytes were to be read then the pointer would be set to 9100. The offset pointer is also updated and again points to the byte following the last byte to be transferred on the file. The number of bytes value is also changed and the new value represents the number of requested bytes not successfully transferred. If everything has been alright then this value will normally be zero. All these values can be read from the control block and saved for future use by your data handling programs.

The demonstration program will list these values out on the screen. As in the case of the OSFILE routine the data start address must be carefully chosen using a section of memory that is clear of any current Basic or machine code programs. For testing purposes the start address 9000 may be used which is clear of the demonstration program. Note that the actual data start address as specified in the control block will have precedence over any load addresses specified on the file catalog.

It can be seen that by manipulating the data and file offset pointers you can divide the file into a series of fixed length blocks and with simple calculations you can access any of the blocks by changing the value of the offset pointer. For convenience the data pointer would be set to a fixed starting value to enable your program to use a fixed block of memory for its data processing. An example for block data files might be by using the file to hold a mailing list with each block containing the name and address of people with surnames all starting with 'S' and also perhaps having a different data file for every letter of the alphabet.

The next section of the demonstration program concerns the use of OSARGS to read and write the file attributes. Details are given on page 454 of the User Guide. For file processing, the main operations are reading and writing the file offset pointer (or sequential pointer) and reading the total file length. Reading and writing to the sequential pointer using OSARGS is only needed if you are using OSBGET or OSBPUT.

These routines (see p.453 of User Guide) are used for transferring single bytes to and from the file and require the offset pointer being set prior to calling these routines. However, reading the pointer will give the correct value as an alternative to reading the OSGBPB control block. Another use of OSARGS is to read the length of the file to calculate how much space is left on the file for new data.

When using OSARGS, the Y register must contain the file channel number, the A register must be set for the required operation:

A=0   Read sequential pointer

A=1   Write sequential pointer

A=255   'Ensure' file is up to date on the media

For reading and writing to the pointer and reading the file length a group of four bytes in page zero are used for these values. The X register is used to point to the start address of these locations. In the demonstration program locations &80 to &83 are used for this purpose (locations &70 to &8F are available for user purposes).

When running this section of the demonstration program, you are asked to input the value A to determine the operation and after OSARGS has been called the contents of this block of memory will be output showing the value of the pointer or the file length as needed.

The last section of the program contains a routine which can be used to dump a section of memory to the screen. Start and end addresses are requested by the program.

This routine will enable you to examine data in hex form read from the file and by noting these bytes and then by changing the file offset and reloading the data into memory, you should be able to see how the data has been shifted.

Process Program Notes

Lines 70,80 are used to allocate space for the various machine code routines.

Lines 90-110 input the filename and store it starting at location &0DB0.

Lines 120-230 set addresses for OSFIND and CHAN (used to save the channel number). A machine code routine is used to set the X and Y registers to point to a control block starting at &0DB0 and also to set the A register to &C0 for random access operation. On completion of the OSFIND operation, the channel number is obtained from the A register and is stored in &0DE0.

Lines 240-260 call this machine code routine and if the returned channel number is 0 then a 'File not found' message is output, otherwise the channel number assigned to the file is output.

Lines 290-390 input the information required to set up the control block used by OSGBPB setting &0D80 to the channel number, &0D81-0D84 to the data pointer, &0D85-0D88 to the number of bytes to be transferred, and, finally, &0D89 & 0D8C to the file offset.

Lines 400-530 contain the machine code routine to set the A register for the required operation and the X and Y registers to point to a control block at &0D80. When the routine has been called lines 490 to 530 ouput the information returned in the control block.

Lines 550-610 list and request the operation required for use by OSARGS.

Lines 630-710 set the address for OSARGS and has a section of machine code to set the A register for the required operation, and sets the X register to point to a control block in page zero of memory (&80). Note that locations &70 to &8F are available to the user.

Lines 720-740 call the machine code and on completion the sequential pointer or file length are returned in the control block and then output to the screen for operations with A=0, 1 or 2.

Line 750 is used to close the opened file once finished with. This will enable the file to be reopened if the demonstration program is run and the same file requested. In general, files must be closed otherwise access by other routines or programs will cause a 'File already open' error.

Lines 760-910 contain the memory dumper routine which inputs the required start and end addresses in decimal and then using a FOR loop, 'pokes' each required location and outputs to the screen.

The format used is to print the start address of a group of eight bytes in decimal and then list each byte in hex as one row. This is repeated for each group of bytes. Line 840 selects the print format for the decimal address by selecting 'fixed format', '0 decimal places' and a '4 character field' (this also sets the display of the hex bytes).

```
>L.10,450
   10  REM DEMO FOR FILE MANIPULATION
   20  REM USING OSFIND, OSARGS, OSGBPB
   30  REM M.Sein - Computer Users Club
   40  MODE 7
   50  PRINT'"XXDISC FILE PROCESSING DEMOXX"
   60  PRINT
   70  DIM MEM 100
   80  P%=MEM
   90  INPUT"Filename?"F$
  100  F=&0DB0
  110  $F=F$
  120  OSFIND=&FFCE
  130  CHAN=&0DE0
  140  REM XXSET UP OSFIND
  150  [OPT0
  160  .FIND
  170  LDA #&C0\Set for Random Access
  180  LDX #&B0\Set filename pointer
  190  LDY #&0D\Set filename pointer
  200  JSR OSFIND
  210  STA CHAN\Save channel no.
  220  RTS
  230  ]
  240  CALL FIND
  250  IF ?CHAN=0 THEN PRINT"File not found":CLOSE£0:END
  260  PRINT"Channel no.(hex)= ";~?CHAN
  270  PRINT
  280  REM XXPROCESS OPENED FILE
  290  OSGBPB=&FFD1
  300  INPUT"Read or Write reqd (R/W)? "S$
  310  IF S$="R" THEN OP=3 ELSE IF S$="W"THEN OP=1 ELSE 300
  320  REM XXSET UP OSGBPB CONTROL BLOCK
  330  INPUT"Mem Pointer Start Addr(dec) "TRANS%
  340  INPUT"No. of bytes to transfer(dec) "BYTE%
  350  INPUT"File pointer(File Offset) (dec) "SET%
  360  ?&0D80=?CHAN
  370  !&0D81=TRANS%
  380  !&0D85=BYTE%
  390  !&0D89=SET%
  400  [OPT0
  410  .PRO
  420  LDA #OP\Set for Read or Write
  430  LDX #&80\Set Ctrl Blk pointer
  440  LDY #&0D\Set Ctrl Blk pointer
  450  JSR OSGBPB
```

```
>L.460.
  460  RTS
  470  ]
  480  CALL PRO
  490  REM XXOUTPUT RESULTS IN CONTROL BLOCK
  500  PRINT''INFO RETURNED IN CTRL BLOCK"
  510  PRINT"New mem pointer value(hex) ";~!&0D81
  520  PRINT"No. of bytes not transferred(hex) ";~!&0D85
  530  PRINT"New file pointer value(hex) ";~!&0D89
  540  REM XXOSARGS DEMO
  550  PRINT''XXEXAMINE FILE ATTRIBUTES - OSARGSXX"
  560  PRINT"Select Operation Read:"
  570   PRINT"Read Sequential Pointer(A=0)"
  580  PRINT"Write Sequential Pointer(A=1)"
  590  PRINT"Read File Length(A=2)"
  600  PRINT"Ensure File is up to date(A=255)"
  610  INPUT"A= "OP
  620  IF OP=1 THEN INPUT"Sequential File Pointer value(dec) "IND%:!&80=IND%
  630  OSARGS=&FFDA
  640  [OPT0
  650  .ARG
  660  LDA £OP\Set operation
  670  LDX £&80\Point to control block
  680  LDY CHAN\Set channel no.
  690  JSR OSARGS
  700  RTS
  710  ]
  720  CALL ARG
  730  IF OP=0 OR OP=1 THEN PRINT''Sequential Pointer(hex) ";~!&80
  740  IF OP=2 THEN PRINT''File Length(hex) ";~!&80
  750  CLOSE£0
  760  REM XXMEMORY DUMPERXX
  770  PRINT
  780  INPUT"Do you wish to examine memory(Y/N)?"S$
  790  IF S$="N" THEN END
  800  PRINT''XXMEMORY DUMPERXX"
  810  INPUT"Start Address(dec):"R
  820  INPUT"End Address(dec):"E
  830  PRINT
  840  @%=&00020004
  850  PRINT R:
  860  FOR J=1 TO 8
  870    PRINT~?R:
  880    R=R+1
  890    NEXT J
  900  PRINT:IF R=E OR R>E THEN END ELSE 850
  910  END
```

In conclusion, the preceding programs should have demonstrated how files may be processed and the machine code routines can form the basis of larger data handling programs with the information for the operation and setting of the control blocks being derived automatically by the data handling program.

Program Listings

The program listings which follow are computer printouts of the actual working programs, as opposed to a typeset list. This is done in order to eliminate errors. At the top of each page the line may be seen calling a section of the program to be listed e.g.

L.10,450

This of course should not be typed when you enter the program into your computer.

The dot matrix printer used to provide the listings was factory set to reproduce English characters as opposed to American or Spanish. This means that certain keys would produce different symbols for each language. The main difference demanding care from the user is the HASH symbol # which is shown as # on the keyboard but produces £ when printed using the English setting.

Throughout the programs which follow, where you read £ you should type # .

7 Useful Programs

Disk Formatting and Verifying

Floppy disk are used for mass storage of programs and data which can be accessed very much faster than cassette tapes. This is possible by having the facility to rotate the disk at high speed (typically 300 revolutions per minute) which means that data can be read to and from the disk at high speed, typically 125,000 bits per second, which, compared with tape transfer (1200 bits per second) is very much faster.

Data is recorded on the disk as a series of concentric rings called 'tracks' and each track is sub-divided into sections called 'sectors'.

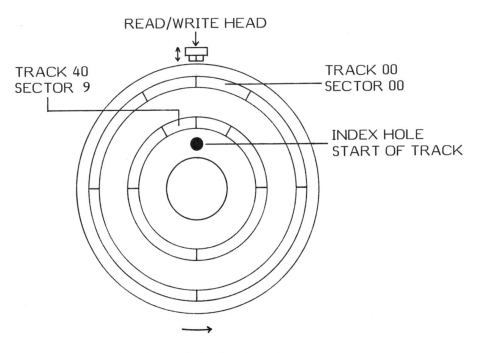

Fig. 7.1 Track Layout

Access to the data is achieved by allowing the record and playback head to move radially across the disk to access a particular track and then read the track and search for the required sector. This contrasts with the tape system where the tape must be searched starting at the beginning of the tape or the approximate position where a program is expected to be found. The disk therefore has the advantage of being able to skip very quickly over tracks that are not required to the specific track where the data is expected to be found.

Considering disks in use, these are normally blank and therefore have to be pre-recorded with the track and sector patterns before they can be used for data storage. This pre-recording is done using a formatting program which can be held in a Read Only Memory, or in the case of the BBC Computer, held as a program on a formatting disk.

The number of tracks vary between disk drives and are normally 35, 40 or 80 tracks for 'mini' Floppy Disks which we are discussing here. The number of sectors on the tracks can vary between one sector (taking up the entire track) to eighteen. The BBC disk system caters for 40 and 80 track drives with tracks divided into ten sectors as standard, but the formatting program to be described will enable 35 track drives to be used as well.

As the track contains many sectors, there has to be a way in which the computer can search the track to find the sector or sectors required. This is done by dividing each sector into two parts:

a)   A sector IDentifier called an 'ID field'

b)   A data field which contains the stored data.

The ID field contains pre-recorded information (recorded by formatting):

i)   A unique byte which identifies the field as an ID field (&FE)

ii)   the track address (a number between 0 and 39/79 for 40 or 80 track disks)

iii)   A 'side' number which is &00 for single sided disks or &01 for the second side of a double sided disk

iv)   The actual sector address (a number between 0 and 9)

v)   A value (2) indicating the length of the data field (in multiples of 128 bytes giving a total of 256 bytes)

and finally,

vi)   Two Cyclic Redundancy Check bytes which are used for error checking in a similar way to which the cassette system checks for tape error.

Sector 00 Track 00

Sector 00 Track 00 contains the following information.

	A	B	C	B1	C1	etc
&00	&08	&0F	&10	&1F	&20	

BYTES

A Consists of 8 bytes, being the start of the disk title (12 chrs).
B Starts with &08 and contains the first filename.
C Contains a directory letter for the first file. (bit 7 is set if file is locked).
B1 Second filename starting &10
C1 Second directory letter.

The process continues for a maximum of 31 filenames.

Sector 01 Track 00

Sector 01 Track 00 contains the following information.

	D	D1	E	F	F	H	I
&00	&04	&05	&06	&07	&08	&09	

D The 4 remaining bytes of the disk title.
D1 Number of disk access operations (hex).
D A value which is the number of catalog entries times 8, i.e. catalog pointer (beginning of last file entry).
F Contains a value for the number of sectors on the disk (2 high bits,[0,1] bits 4 & 5 are !BOOT option flag).
G Contains the 8 low bits of a 10 bit number giving the number of sectors on the disk.
H First file load address (lo bits).
I First file load address (middle bits).

Sector 01 Track 00 (Cont.)

J	K	L	M	N	0 etc.
&0A	&0B	&0C	&0D	&0E	&0F

J First file execution address (low bits).
K First file execution address (middle bits).
L First file length (low bits).
M First file length (middle bits).
N a) First file start sector (2 high bits of a 10 bit
   number) - bits 0,1.
   b) First file load address (high bits) = bits 2,3.
   c) First file length (high bits) - bits 4,5.
   d) First file execution address (high bits) - bits 6,7.
0 First file start sector (8 low bits of a 10 bit number).

The process continues for a maximum of 31 filenames.

Zero Page File address etc.

H	=	&BE
I	=	&BF
J	=	&C0
K	=	&C1
L	=	&C2
M	=	&C3
N	=	&C4
O	=	&C5

In this way, once the read/write head is positioned over
the correct track, the sector ID fields can be read to find
the one required and then the data field immediately
following that particular ID field may read or be written
to.

The format of the information recorded on the ID
and Data fields has been standardized to allow disks from
different types of computers to be interchanged as far as
reading or writing to specific sectors is concerned,
although the actual processing of the information is

determined by individual disk operating systems and these are not generally compatible.

This standardization was laid down when the 8" floppy disks were developed and was referred to as the IBM3740 Soft Sector format, and with the introduction of 'mini' floppies ($5\frac{1}{4}$") this IBM format formed the basis of a new standard.

The similarity between the standards has allowed hardware disk controller IC's developed for 8" drives to be used with mini floppy drives as in the case of the BBC machine. This simplifies the software control of the drives as the 8271 controller IC used in the BBC machine can accept specific commands such as READ, WRITE, FORMAT and VERIFY TRACK issued by the operating system, and therefore generate all the necessary 'housekeeping' signals by itself and only interrupts the processor when it has finished its current command.

In order to format a blank disk all the ID fields and Data field must be pre-recorded with dummy data and then a file catalog must be set up to enable the File Operating System to correctly access the disk.

The BBC Disk Filing System uses sectors 00 and 01 on track 00 for the catalog as previously mentioned.

To prepare the catalog for use, all filenames and the various addresses may be set to 00. Thus sector 00 may be set to all 00s and sector 01 may be set to 00s apart from the seventh and eighth byte which is used to store the 10 bit number representing the total number of sectors on the disk.

This number is used to enable the Disk File System to know when the disk is full and is also used by the verifier program to calculate the number of tracks recorded on a disk. The number recorded is:

&0190	(400 sectors)	for 40 track disks.
&0320	(800 sectors)	for 80 track disks.
&015E	(350 sectors)	for 35 track disks.

Thus to format the disk, the tracks and sectors addresses must be supplied to the controller IC and then when all tracks have been formatted, the catalog is then written to the first two sectors in track 00.

Going on to consider in more detail the exact bytes recorded on each track, see the following diagram:

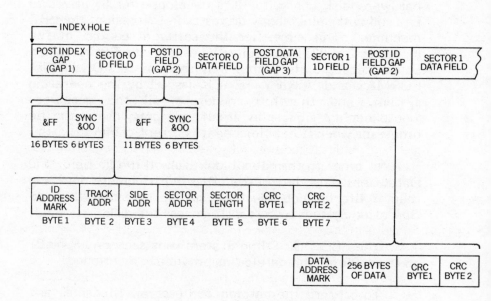

Fig. 7.2 Details of Gaps and Fields

As can be seen, there are various gaps separating the ID fields and Data fields. These 'gaps' are bytes which are used for synchronizing the disk controller ready for reading the serial data on the disk. The method used in recording data on the disk is called 'Frequency Modulation' where a continuous train of pulses are recorded (these being called clock pulses), with the serial data interleaved between the clock pulses. In this way a '1' bit is recorded as two pulses and an '0' bit is recorded as a single pulse.

The 'gap' bytes are used to enable external hardware i.e. disk controller and associated logic time to lock on to the clock pulses and to be correctly synchronized to enable the actual serial data pulse train to be separated from the composite pulses.

From Fig. 7.2 the first gap occurs immediately following the index hole. This is a hole punched in the disk and is detected optically by the drive to specify the start of each track. Gap 1 consists of 16 bytes of &FF and 6 synchronizing bytes of &00. This gap is then followed by the ID field which has already been described earlier, and again there is another gap (gap 2) which consists of 11 bytes of &FF and six bytes of &00. There next follows the Data Field which consists of a unique code to identify the field as data and the actual 256 bytes of data followed by the two error detection CRC bytes and, finally, a gap (gap 3) of 21 bytes of &FF and six bytes of &00 to end the first sector.

Subsequent sectors are a repeat of the above starting with gap 2 onwards, and at the end of the tenth sector there is a final gap (gap 4) of approximately thirty bytes of &FF. This gap can vary between drives depending on minor differences in speeds between drives and is thus used to fill up the rest of the tracks until the index hole in the disk is reached again.

Therefore formatting involves recording identifier fields signifying the track address, side number, unique sector address, data length, together with error check bytes and the sector data field of 256 bytes of &E5 dummy data bytes (this being standard to identify that the IBM 3740 format has been used) and is repeated for every track on the disk. IBM is the registered trading name of International Business Machines Ltd.

The following are combined Basic and 6502 Assembler Code programs which use the BBC Operating System routines to transmit hardware commands direct to the 8271 Disk Controller IC for

a)   formatting tracks on blank disks and

b)   performing track verifications on already formatted disks for checking for any format or data corruptions.

Disk Formatter Overall Operation

Studying the program listing supplied at the end of the chapter, the program is divided into three sections.

i)   A section of Basic which inputs parameters such as disk drive number required and number of tracks to be formatted (35,40 or 80).

ii)   A section of machine code program which is assembled and performs the actual disk formatting, and:

iii) another section of Basic which outputs the results of the formatting, such as the number of Format or Verify errors which occurred.

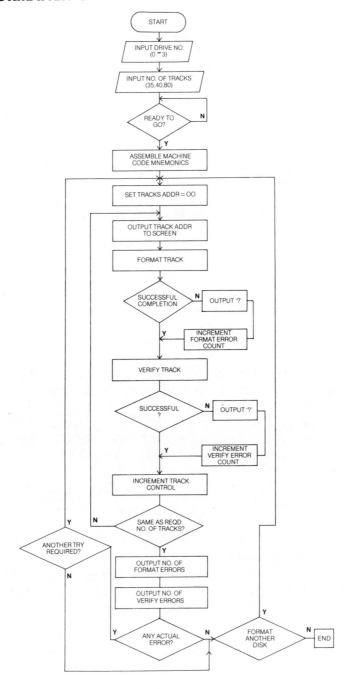

Fig. 7.3 Flowchart of Format Program

Line 60,70 clear the screen and set up Mode 7 then switches off the page mode option.

Lines 80 to 120 prompt the user to input the drive no. and the number of tracks to be formatted. Depending on the "drive no. required", variable DRS% is set to either a '1' or '0' to indicate side 0 or side 1 when double sided drives are being used. When using dual double sided drives, drive no. 0 or 1 represent side 0 for each drive and drive nos. 2 and 3 represent side 1 for each drive.

If only one drive is being used, i.e. drive 0 or 2 (for double sided drives), the user is reminded to remove the formatting disk to avoid re-formatting it, thus losing all programs.

Lines 130 to 150 are used to set up variable HIS%, LOS% which make up the ten bit number which represents the total number of sectors on the disk, either 350 (35 track), 400 (40 tracks) or 800 (80 tracks).

Lines 180 to 260 are used to initialize various parameters which have been allocated specific memory locations. These are the starting track address (Initialized to &00), the drive no. required (DRI%), the number of sectors on each track (TSECT), the side no. (SIDE), the number of track required (TRACK), the number of format errors (FERR), the number of verify errors (VERR), the total number of sectors on the disk (LOS%,HIS%).

Lines 270 to 2820 set up a loop which is used to go through the assembly code lines twice to complete the generation of machine code starting at location set by P%. P% is used to represent the 6502 program counter which points to the next address to be handled.

Lines 290 to 400 contain the list of variables used in the assembly program and their allocated memory addresses.

Lines 410 and 420 indicate the start of the assembly code and the OPT function suppresses error and listing during the first pass through the code, and suppresses listing and reports errors, if any, during the second pass through the code.

Line 440 calls the routine IDFIELD which sets up a block of data in memory which must be sent to the disk controller during the formatting process for each track.

Line 450 calls DCHAR which outputs the track number about to be formatted to the screen.

Line 460 calls the routine CMDPAR which sets up a block of data in memory which contains parameters required to signify the drive to be formatted and the actual format command and parameters required to be transmitted to the controller. This block of data is accessed when the operating system OSWORD routine is called to handle access to the disk controller.

Lines 470 to 500 call the OSWORD routine where the accumulator is set to &7F to signify that a read/write disk operation is required and the X,Y registers are set to point to the start of the block of data (in this case &3F80) required by the OSWORD routine.

Lines 510 to 570 are used to process the result of the formatting operation. When the command is completed an 'error' code is returned at the end of the data block by the OSWORD routine. In the case of a successful completion, the code returned is &00. If the result is &00 then lines 540 to 570 are skipped over. If the result is non-zero then the format error counter FERR is incremented and a '?' is outputted to the screen using the OSASCI routine.

Lines 590 to 600 are used to output a 'space' to the screen if the command is successful.

Line 620 calls the routine VER which again sets up a block of data in memory containing information required to set up a verification command to check that the track just formatted does not contain any corrupted information.

Lines 630 to 760 call the OSWORD routine to action the verify operation and similar to the format command, an error byte is returned on completion. If an error has occurred, a '?' is output to the screen, and the verify error counter VERR is incremented. If no error occurs then a 'space' is output to the screen.

Lines 770 to 810 increment the current track address and check the value against the total number of tracks to be formatted (TCOUNT). If the incremented address does not match with TCOUNT, then the program loops back to START to format the next track.

Line 820 calls DIRDATA routine which sets up the data required to format the two sectors of track 00 as previously described.

Line 830 calls the routine DIRINIT which sets up a block of data with command parameters at location &3F A0 onwards prior to calling OSWORD in lines 840 to 870.

Lines 880 to 910 deal with checking if any errors occurred. FERR error counter is incremented if any error has occurred.

Lines 920 to 950 are used to reset the track address to &00 and calls routine VER to set up the data block containing the parameter for a verification command for checking the newly written catalog sector.

Lines 960 to 1030 execute the verify command and check for errors, incrementing the error counter VERR if necessary.

Finally, line 1050 executes a return to Basic to carry on with the remaining parts of the main program.

The following lines (1060-2550) contain the routines for setting the blocks of data required when sending commands via OSWORD to the disk controller.

In all these routines absolute indexed addressing is used with the base address fixed and sequential locations accessed by incrementing the X register.

Lines 1060 to 1450 set up the track format command with the following byte:

&3F80	DRIVE	Drive No.
&3F81	&BO	Data address lo byte
&3F82	&3F	Data address hi byte
&3F83	&00	Data address hi byte
&3F84	&00	Data address hi byte
&3F85	&05	No. of command parameters
&3F86	&63	Disk Controller Format command byte
&3F87	TRACK	Track address
&3F88	&15	Gap 3 size (21 bytes)
&3F89	&2A	Sector length/no. of sectors (256 bytes/10 sectors)
&3F8A	&00	Gap 5 size (0 byte)
&3F8B	&10	Gap 1 size (16 bytes)
&3F8C	&FF	Dummy error code

Lines 1460 to 1770 set up the verify track command:

&3F90	DRIVE	Drive no.
&3F91	&00	Dummy data address
&3F92	&00	Dummy data address
&3F93	&00	Dummy data address
&3F94	&00	Dummy data address
&3F95	&03	No. of command parameters
&3F96	&5F	Disk Controller Verify command byte
&3F97	TRACK	Track address
&3F98	&00	Sector start address
&3F99	&2A	Sector length/no. of sectors (256 bytes/10 sectors)
&3F9A	&FF	Dummy error code

Lines 1780 to 2100 set up the write command for the two catalog sectors:

&3FA0	DRIVE	Drive no.
&3FA1	&00	Data address lo byte
&3FA2	&40	Data address hi byte
&3FA3	&00	Data address hi byte
&3FA4	&00	Data address hi byte
&3FA5	&03	No. of command parameters
&3FA6	&4B	Disk Controller write command byte
&3FA7	&00	Track address
&3FA8	&00	Sector start address
&3FA9	&22	Sector length/no. of sectors (256 bytes/2 sectors)
&3FAA	&FF	Dummy error code

Lines 2110 to 2300 contain the routine for setting up the data required by the disk controller format command routine CMDPAR. The format command requires the ID field byte for each sector to be transmitted to the disk controller during formatting. This routine produces ten sets of ID fields each consisting of the track address (TRACK), side no. (SIDE), sector address, sector length.

Lines 2310 to 2550 contain the routine DIRDATA, for setting up the data to be recorded on the two catalog sectors:

&4000 - &40FF	256 bytes of &00 (Sector 00)
&4100 - &4105	6 bytes of &00
&4106	High byte of disk size (HISIZE)
&4107	Lo byte of disk size (LOSIZE)
&4108 - &41FF	248 bytes of &00

Finally, lines 2560 to 2800 are concerned with outputting the address of each track as it is formatted.

The address to be output is held in the A register after being loaded from location TRACK. It is also temporarily stored in the Y register (line 2580). As the address must be displayed as two ASCII hex characters, the upper four bits of A must be converted to ASCII first.

Lines 2600 to 2630, the upper four bits are rotated right into the lower four bit position of the A register. Line 2650 AND's the A register with &0F which sets the upper four bits to 00 while leaving the lower four bits intact. Line 2660 sets the carry flag and line 2670 subtracts &0A from the accumulator to test whether a number or letter is required. If the result of the subtract is negative, i.e. a number, the carry flag is reset and line 2890 adds &0A to the A register to recover the original number before the subtraction operation and then &30 to convert it to ASCII (Numbers 0-9 are represented by codes &30-&39).

If however, the result is positive, the carry flag remains set and a jump to TX1 is made where line 2720 adds &0A to recover the original number and &36 to convert it to an ASCII character (Letters A-F are represented by codes &41-&46).

With the ASCII code for the number or letter in the A register, line 2740 calls the operating system OSASCI routine which outputs the character to the screen. The character counter (X register) is then incremented and if the second character has been output, then a return is made to the main assembly routine. If another character is needed, the A register is reloaded with the original two digit number and a jump to CHAR2 (line 2640) for conversion and outputting to screen.

This completes the operation of the assembly code and there just remains the third section of the main Basic program, lines 2830 to 2960. These call the assembled machine code stored at &3200 and after formatting is complete, output the contents of FERR and VERR which contain the number of errors found during the format process. If any errors have occurred, line 2900 prompts the user to see if another try is wanted at formatting the failed disk.

If so, TRACK, FERR and VERR are re-initialized to &00 and a jump is made back to line 2830 to repeat the formatting process. Assuming a format operation has been successfully completed, the user is prompted to see if another disk needs formatting using the same drive. If so the user is prompted to insert another blank disk and then TRACK, FERR, and VERR are set to 00 and a jump made to line 2830 and off the program goes again.

A typical run is shown below:

DRIVE No. ?0

REMOVE FORMAT DISK

Insert blank disk into drive 0
No. of tracks required (80,40,35) ?40
Ready to format drive (Y/N)?   Y

3200
3200

Formatting Drive 0 - Please wait

00	01	02	03	04	05	06	07	08	09
0A	0B	0C	0D	0E	0F	10	11	12	13
14	15	16	17	18	19	1A	1B	1C	1D
1E	1F	20	21	22	23	24	25	26	27

Drive 0 formatting complete

0 Format error
0 Verify error

Format another disk (Y/N)?

```
>L.10,450
  10 REM DISC FORMATTER V2.0
  20 REM Copyright (C) M. Sein B.Sc(hons) 1982
  30 REM Computer Users Club
  40 REM Modifications by Tony Latham
  60 MODE7
  70 VDU15
  80 INPUT"Drive No.?"DRI%
  90 IF DRI%=0 OR DRI%=2 THEN PRINT"REMOVE FORMAT DISK"
 100  IF DRI%=0 OR DRI%=1 THEN DRS%=0 ELSE IF DRI%=2
     OR DRI%=3 THEN DRS%=1 ELSE80
 110 PRINT:PRINTCHR$(130)" Insert blank disk into drive ";DRI%
 120 INPUT"No. of tracks required (80,40,35)?"TRA%
 130 IF TRA%=35THEN LOS%=&5E:HIS%=&01:GOTO160
 140 IF TRA%=40THEN LOS%=&90:HIS%=&01:GOTO160
 150 IF TRA%=80THEN LOS%=&20:HIS%=&03:GOTO160ELSE120
 160 INPUT"Ready to format drive(Y/N)?"A$
 170 IFA$="N"THEN END ELSE IF A$<>"Y"THEN 160
 180 ?&3F9D=0
 190 ?&3F9F=DRI%
 200 ?&3F9B=10
 210 ?&3F9C=DRS%
 220 ?&3FAF=TRA%
 230 ?&3FAE=0
 240 ?&3FAD=0
 250 ?&3FAB=LOS%
 260 ?&3FAC=HIS%
 270 FOR X=0 TO 2STEP2
 280    P%=&3200
 290    OSWORD=&FFF1
 300    OSASCI=&FFE3
 310    TCOUNT=&3FAF
 320    TSECT=&3F9B
 330    FERR=&3FAE
 340    VERR=&3FAD
 350    DRIVE1=&3F9E
 360    DRIVE=&3F9F
 370    TRACK=&3F9D
 380    SIDE=&3F9C
 390    LOSIZE=&3FAB
 400    HISIZE=&3FAC
 410    [
 420    OPT X
 430    .START
 440    JSR IDFIELD\Set format data
 450    JSR DCHAR
```

```
>L.460,900
  460 JSR CMDPAR\Set up Format cmd
  470 LDA £&7F
  480 LDX £&80
  490 LDY £&3F
  500 JSR OSWORD
  510 LDA &3F8C\Get error code
  520 CMP £0
  530 BEQ LPV1\Jump if OK
  540 INC FERR\Incr error count
  550 LDA £&3F
  560 JSR OSASCI\Output '?'
  570 JMP LPV2
  580 .LPV1
  590 LDA £&20
  600 JSR OSASCI\Output 'space'
  610 .LPV2
  620 JSR VER\Set up verify command
  630 LDA £&7F
  640 LDX £&90
  650 LDY £&3F
  660 JSR OSWORD
  670 LDA &3F9A\Get error code
  680 CMP £0
  690 BEQ LPV3\Jump if OK
  700 INC VERR\Incr error count
  710 LDA £&3F
  720 JSR OSASCI\Output '?'
  730 JMP LPV4
  740 .LPV3
  750 LDA £&20
  760 JSR OSASCI\Output 'space'
  770 .LPV4
  780 INC TRACK
  790 LDA TRACK\Get new track addr
  800 CMP TCOUNT\Check with disc size
  810 BNE START\Loop if not finished
  820 JSR DIRDATA\Set-up directory data
  830 JSR DIRINIT\Set-up directory cmd
  840 LDA £&7F
  850 LDX £&A0
  860 LDY £&3F
  870 JSR OSWORD
  880 LDA &3FAA\Get error code
  890 CMP £0
  900 BEQ LPV5\Jump if OK
```

```
>L.910,1350
  910 INC FERR
  920 .LPV5
  930 LDA £00
  940 STA TRACK
  950 JSR VER\Set verify cmd
  960 LDA £&7F
  970 LDX £&90
  980 LDY £&3F
  990 JSR OSWORD
 1000 LDA &3F9A\Get error code
 1010 CMP £0
 1020 BEQ LPV6\Jump if OK
 1030 INC VERR\Inc error count
 1040 .LPV6
 1050 RTS\Return to BASIC
 1060 .CMDPAR
 1070 LDX £00
 1080 LDA DRIVE
 1090 STA &3F80,X\ Save drive no.
 1100 INX
 1110 LDA £&B0
 1120 STA &3F80,X\ Save lo data addr
 1130 INX
 1140 LDA £&3F
 1150 STA &3F80,X\ Save hi data addr
 1160 INX
 1170 LDA £00
 1180 STA &3F80.X\Save hi-hi addr
 1190 INX
 1200 STA &3F80.X
 1210 INX
 1220 LDA £&05
 1230 STA &3F80.X\Save no. of cmd pars
 1240 INX
 1250 LDA £&63\Set format cmd
 1260 STA &3F80.X
 1270 INX
 1280 LDA TRACK\Get track addr
 1290 STA &3F80.X
 1300 INX
 1310 LDA £21
 1320 STA &3F80.X\Save Gap3 size
 1330 INX
 1340 LDA £&2A
 1350 STA &3F80.X\Save length/sector nos
```

```
>L.1360,1800
 1360 INX
 1370 LDA £00
 1380 STA &3F80,X\Save Gap5(0 bytes)
 1390 INX
 1400 LDA £&10
 1410 STA &3F80,X\Save Gap1 size
 1420 INX
 1430 LDA £&FF
 1440 STA &3F80,X\Save dummy error code
 1450 RTS
 1460 .VER \Set verify cmd pars
 1470 LDX £00
 1480 LDA DRIVE
 1490 STA &3F90,X\Save drive no.
 1500 INX
 1510 LDA £&00
 1520 STA &3F90,X\Save dummy data addr
 1530 INX
 1540 STA &3F90,X
 1550 INX
 1560 STA &3F90,X
 1570 INX
 1580 STA &3F90,X
 1590 INX
 1600 LDA £&03
 1610 STA &3F90,X\Save no.of cmd pars
 1620 INX
 1630 LDA £&5F\Set verify cmd
 1640 STA &3F90,X\Save verify cmd
 1650 INX
 1660 LDA TRACK
 1670 STA &3F90,X\Save track addr
 1680 INX
 1690 LDA £00
 1700 STA &3F90,X\Save sector start
 1710 INX
 1720 LDA £&2A
 1730 STA &3F90,X\Save length/sector nos
 1740 INX
 1750 LDA £&FF
 1760 STA &3F90,X\Save dummy error code
 1770 RTS
 1780 .DIRINIT
 1790 LDX£0
 1800 LDA DRIVE
```

```
>L.1810,2250
 1810 STA &3FA0\Save drive no.
 1820 INX
 1830 LDA £&00
 1840 STA &3FA0,X\Save lo data addr
 1850 INX
 1860 LDA £&40
 1870 STA &3FA0,X\Save hi data
 1880 INX
 1890 LDA £00
 1900 STA &3FA0,X\Save hi-hi addr
 1910 INX
 1920 STA &3FA0,X
 1930 INX
 1940 LDA £03
 1950 STA &3FA0,X\Save no. of pars
 1960 INX
 1970 LDA £&4B\Set Write cmd
 1980 STA &3FA0,X\Save complete cmd
 1990 INX
 2000 LDA £00
 2010 STA &3FA0,X\Save track addr
 2020 INX
 2030 STA &3FA0,X\Save sector start addr
 2040 INX
 2050 LDA £&22
 2060 STA &3FA0,X\Save length/sector nos
 2070 INX
 2080 LDA £&FF
 2090 STA &3FA0,X\Save dummy error code
 2100 RTS
 2110 .IDFIELD
 2120 LDY £00\Set sector counter
 2130 LDX £00
 2140 .LOOP
 2150 LDA TRACK\Get track addr
 2160 STA &3FB0,X
 2170 INX
 2180 LDA SIDE\Get side no.
 2190 STA &3FB0,X
 2200 INX
 2210 TYA\Get sector no.
 2220 STA &3FB0,X
 2230 INX
 2240 LDA £01\Set sector length
 2250 STA &3FB0,X
```

```
>L.2260,2700
 2260 INX
 2270 INY
 2280 CPY TSECT\Last sector?
 2290 BNE LOOP
 2300 RTS
 2310 .DIRDATA
 2320 LDY £&FF\Set loop counter
 2330 LDX £00
 2340 .DLP1
 2350 LDA £00\Set data byte
 2360 STA &4000,X
 2370 INX
 2380 DEY
 2390 TYA
 2400 CMP £00
 2410 BNE DLP1
 2420 LDY £&FF
 2430 .DLP2
 2440 LDA £00\Set data byte
 2450 STA &4100,X
 2460 INX
 2470 DEY
 2480 TYA
 2490 CMP £00
 2500 BNE DLP2
 2510 LDA HISIZE
 2520 STA &4106\Set hi disc size
 2530 LDA LOSIZE
 2540 STA &4107\Set lo disc size
 2550 RTS
 2560 .DCHAR
 2570 LDA TRACK
 2580 TAY\Save in Y
 2590 LDX £&FE\Set char counter
 2600 ROR A
 2610 ROR A
 2620 ROR A
 2630 ROR A
 2640 .CHAR2
 2650 AND £&0F\Mask top nibble
 2660 SEC\Set carry for subtraction
 2670 SBC £&0A\Separate letter/number
 2680 BCS TX1\Carry set=letter A-F
 2690 ADC £&3A\Convert no. to ASCII
 2700 BCS TX2
```

```
>L.2710,
 2710 .TX1
 2720 ADC £&40\Convert letter to ASCII
 2730 .TX2
 2740 JSR OSASCI
 2750 INX\Another nibble
 2760 BEQ TX3\Jump if finished
 2770 TYA\Recover byte
 2780 JMP CHAR2
 2790 .TX3
 2800 RTS
 2810 ]
 2820  NEXT X
 2830  PRINT"Formatting Drive ";DRI%;" -Please wait"
 2840 PRINT
 2850 CALL&3200
 2860 PRINT
 2870 PRINT"Drive ";DRI%;" formatting complete"
 2880 PRINT ?FERR;" Format errors"
 2890 PRINT ?VERR;" Verify errors"
 2900  IF?FERR<>0 OR ?VERR<>0 THEN
      INPUT"Another try(Y/N)?"A$:GOTO2930
 2910 INPUT"Format another disk(Y/N)?"A$
 2920 IF A$="Y"THEN2940 ELSE END
 2930  IF A$="N"THEN2910 ELSE IF A$="Y"THEN ?TRACK=0:
      ?FERR=0:?VERR=0:GOTO2830 ELSE END
 2940 PRINT:PRINTCHR$(130)" Insert blank disc into drive ";DRI%
 2950 INPUT"Ready to format drive(Y/N)?"A$
 2960 IFA$="Y"THEN?TRACK=0:?FERR=0:?VERR=0:GOTO2830 ELSE END
```

Disk Verifying

This program is used to check disks that have already been formatted and in use for some time for any corruptions or drop-outs in the ID and data fields.

'Drop ins' are spurious bits of bytes written during power surges and spikes of the Mains voltages or program errors. 'Drop outs' are bits, bytes or words that have for one reason or another been accidentally erased.

A flowchart for the program is shown in Fig. 7.4.

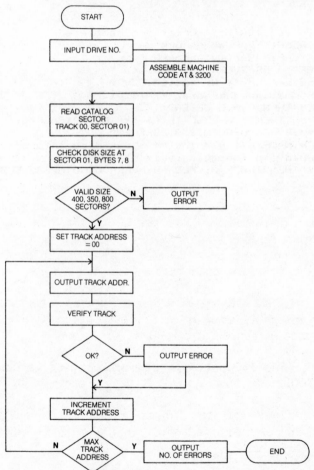

Fig. 7.4 Flowchart of Verify Program

Similar to the format program, this program is divided into three sections.

i) A section of Basic inputting the drive number to be checked and initializing the variables used.

ii) A section of machine code program which is assembled and which performs the actual verification, and

iii) another section of Basic which outputs the result of the verification.

Lines 35 and 36 clear the screen, set up Mode 7 and switch off the page mode option.

Line 40 prompts the user to input the drive number required.

Lines 50 to 70 check that the drive number is valid i.e. 0-3 and prompts the user to start the verification.

Lines 90 to 120 are used to initialize memory locations allocated for holding the various parameters which are used by the Basic section of the program and the machine code. These locations represent VERR (verify error counter), TRACK, DERR (Directory error), DRIVE (current drive no.).

Lines 130 and 1870 form a loop which runs through the assembly code lines twice to generate the machine code to be stored at &3200.

Line 140 sets the program counter variable P% to &3200.

Lines 150 to 230 assign name variables to the special memory locations which will be used in the assembly code.

Lines 260 and 270 start by calling the routine DIRCMD which sets a block of data in memory with parameters required to perform a READ command on track 0, sector 01.

Lines 280 to 310 set the A register for disk controller access, also register X and Y to point to the data block at &2FA0 (set up by the DIRCMD routine) and call the operating system routine OSWORD which then performs the read operations.

Line 320 reads the error code returned by OSWORD. If the code isn't &00 then DERR is incremented and the program continues.

Lines 370 to 430 examine byte 7 of the catalog sector which should contain the high two bits of the ten bit disk size number. The byte is logically ANDed with &03 to mask off the upper six bits. This byte is checked to see if it is either &01 (representing 40 or 35 track disk) or &03 (80 track disk). If neither of these two then DERR is incremented and an immediate return to Basic is made. Depending upon the value of the byte a jump is made to either DS1 or DS2 to check for the correct low byte size.

Lines 440 to 510 examine byte 8 and check whether it is &90 (40 track disk) or &5E (35 track disk). If the byte is &90 then a jump is made to DS3 (lines 520-540) which sets TCOUNT with decimal 40, the number of tracks to be verified. If the byte is &5E then a jump is made to DS4 (lines 560-580) which sets TCOUNT with decimal 35, the number of tracks on the disk.

Lines 600 to 650 contain the routine DS2 which checks that the low size byte is &20 for 80 track disk. Again if not, then DERR is incremented and a return to Basic made. If correct, a jump to DS5 (lines 660-680) which sets TCOUNT to decimal 80. Operation then continues with DVER routine.

Line 700 calls DCHAR which outputs the current track address to the screen.

Line 710 calls VER which sets up a block of data at &2F90 for use with lines 720 to 750 which call OSWORD to execute the verify command.

Line 760 gets the error code returned by OSWORD and if the code is &00, a jump to DV2 is made (lines 850-880) which outputs two 'spaces' to the screen using the OSASCI operating system routine.

If however an error has occurred then a '?' and a 'space' is output to the screen (lines 790-830) and VERR error counter is incremented.

Lines 900 to 940 increment the current track address (TRACK) and compares it with the total number of tracks required to be verified (TCOUNT). If the two are equal then the program jumps back to DVER (line 690) for verification of the next track, otherwise a return to Basic is made.

Lines 950 to 1600 contain the routines DIRCMD and VER which set up data blocks for the read and verify command routine.

The DIRCMD routine sets up the following data:

&2FA0	DRIVE	Drive no.
&2FA1	&00	Lo data address
&2FA2	&31	Hi data address
&2FA3	&00	Hi data address
&2FA4	&00	Hi data address
&2FA5	&03	NO. of command parameters
&2FA6	&53	Disk controller read command
&2FA7	&00	Track address
&2FA8	&01	Sector start address
&2FA9	&21	Sector length/no. of sectors (256 bytes/1 sector)
&2FAA	&FF	Dummy error code

The VERR routine sets up the following data:

&2F90	DRIVE	Drive no.
&2F91	&00	Dummy data address
&2F92	&00	Dummy data address
&2F93	&00	Dummy data address
&2F94	&00	Dummy data address
&2F95	&03	No. of command parameters
&2F96	&5F	Disk controller VERIFY command
&2F97	TRACK	Current track address
&2F97	&00	Sector start address
&2F98	&2A	Sector length/no. of sector (256 bytes/10 sectors)
&2F99	&FF	Dummy error code

Similar to the routines used in the Format program absolute indexed addressing is used with the base address fixed and sequential locations accessed by incrementing the X register.

Lines 1610 to 1850 contain the routine DCHAR which is used to convert and display the current track address on the screen. This routine is identical to that used on the Format program and a full description will be found there.

This completes the operation of the assembly code and there just remains the final section of the Basic program. This calls the assembled machine code stored at &3200 and after verification of the disk has been completed the size of the disk is output (40,35,80 track) and the contents of VERR are output. If any error had occurred during the checking of the disk size recorded in the catalog sector, verification would not be carried out and so a message saying 'Disk not formatted' would be ouput instead.

The fact that the BBC Microcomputer can freely mix Basic program lines and machine code in this manner is a great advantage not available on many machines. It is usual to find formatting programs composed entirely of a machine code program loaded from disk onto a definite area in memory which is how the *FORM 80/40 Acorn format programs work.

Of course you can arrange the assembled code to be saved onto the disk with a (fsp) such as 'FORMAT' and use *FORMAT to load and run the program since any word preceded by an asterisk (*) is seen as a command word, offered around the system and if unrecognized offered to the current filing system. If a machine (assembled) code carries the name, then it is seen effectively as a command.

A typical run of the Verify program is shown below.

DRIVE NO. ? 0

Ready to verify drive (Y/N)? Y

3200
3200

Verifying Drive 0 - Please wait

00	01	02	03	04	05	06	07	08	09
0A	0A	0C	0E	0E	0F	10	11	12	13
14	15	16	17	18	19	1A	1B	1C	1D
1E	1F	20	21	22	23	24	25	26	27

40 Track Disk

Drive 0 verify complete

0 Verify errors

```
>L.10,450
   10   REM DISC VERIFIER V2.0
   20 REM Copyright (C) M.Sein B.Sc(hons) 1982
   30 REM Computer Users Club
   35 MODE7
   36 VDU15
   40 INPUT"Drive No.?"DRI%
   50 IF DRI%=0OR DRI%=1OR DRI%=2OR DRI%=3THEN60 ELSE40
   60 INPUT"Ready to verify drive(Y/N)?"A$
   70 IF A$="N"THEN END ELSE IF A$<>"Y"THEN 60
   90 ?&2FAD=0
  100 ?&2F9D=0
  110 ?&2FAE=0
  120 ?&2F9F=DRI%
  130 FOR X=0TO 2 STEP 2
  140    P%=&3200
  150    OSWORD=&FFF1
  160    OSASCI=&FFE3
  170    VERR=&2FAD
  180    DERR=&2FAE
  190    DRIVE=&2F9F
  200    TRACK=&2F9D
  210    LOSIZE=&2FAB
  220    HISIZE=&2FAC
  230    TCOUNT=&2FAF
  240    [
  250    OPT X
  260    .START
  270    JSR DIRCMD\Set cmd blk
  280    LDA £&7F
  290    LDX £&A0
  300    LDY £&2F
  310    JSR OSWORD\Read directory sector 01
  320    LDA &2FAA\Get error code
  330    CMP £0
  340    BEQ V1\Jump if OK
  350    INC DERR\Incr error count
  360    .V1
  370    LDA &3106\Get hi disc size
  375    AND £&03
  380    CMP £&01
  390    BEQ DS1
  400    CMP £&03
  410    BEQ DS2
  420    INC DERR\Error if not 01 or 03
  430    RTS\Return to BASIC
  440    .DS1
  450    LDA &3107\Get lo disc size
```

```
>L.460,900
  460 CMP £&90
  470 BEQ DS3
  480 CMP £&5E
  490 BEQ DS4
  500 INC DERR\Error if not 90 or 5E
  510 RTS\Return to BASIC
  520 .DS3
  530 LDA £&28\Set 40 tracks
  540 STA TCOUNT
  550 JMP DVER
  560 .DS4
  570 LDA £&23\Set 35 tracks
  580 STA TCOUNT
  590 JMP DVER
  600 .DS2
  610 LDA &3107\Get lo disc size
  620 CMP £&20
  630 BEQ DS5
  640 INC DERR\Incr error count
  650 RTS\Return to BASIC
  660 .DS5
  670 LDA £&50\Set 80 tracks
  680 STA TCOUNT
  690 .DVER
  700 JSR DCHAR
  710 JSR VER\Set up verify cmd
  720 LDA £&7F
  730 LDX £&90
  740 LDY £&2F
  750 JSR OSWORD
  760 LDA &2F9A\Get error code
  770 CMP £0
  780 BEQ DV2\Jump if OK
  790 INC VERR\Incr error count
  800 LDA £&3F
  810 JSR OSASCI\Output '?'
  820 LDA £&20
  830 JSR OSASCI\Output 'space'
  840 JMP DV3
  850 .DV2
  860 LDA £&20
  870 JSR OSASCI\Output a 'space'
  880 JSR OSASCI\Output a 'space'
  890 .DV3
  900 INC TRACK
```

```
>L.910,1350
  910 LDA TRACK\Get new track addr
  920 CMP TCOUNT\Check with disc size
  930 BNE DVER\Loop if not finished
  940 RTS\Return to BASIC
  950 .DIRCMD
  960 LDX £0
  970 LDA DRIVE
  980 STA &2FA0,X\Save drive no.
  990 INX
 1000 LDA £&00
 1010 STA &2FA0,X\Save lo data addr
 1020 INX
 1030 LDA £&31
 1040 STA &2FA0,X\Save hi data addr
 1050 INX
 1060 LDA £0
 1070 STA &2FA0,X\Save hi-hi addr
 1080 INX
 1090 STA &2FA0,X
 1100 INX
 1110 LDA £&03
 1120 STA &2FA0,X\Save no. of pars
 1130 INX
 1140 LDA £&53\Set read cmd
 1150 STA &2FA0,X\Save cmd
 1160 INX
 1170 LDA £0
 1180 STA &2FA0,X\Save track addr
 1190 INX
 1200 LDA £&01
 1210 STA &2FA0,X\Save sector start addr
 1220 INX
 1230 LDA £&21
 1240 STA &2FA0,X\Save length/sector nos.
 1250 INX
 1260 LDA £&FF
 1270 STA &2FA0,X\Save dummy error code
 1280 RTS
 1290 .VER
 1300 LDX £0
 1310 LDA DRIVE
 1320 STA &2F90,X\Save drive no.
 1330 INX
 1340 LDA £0
 1350 STA &2F90,X\Save dummy data addr
```

```
>L.1360,1800
  1360 INX
  1370 STA &2F90,X
  1380 INX
  1390 STA &2F90,X
  1400 INX
  1410 STA &2F90,X
  1420 INX
  1430 LDA £&03
  1440 STA &2F90,X\Save no. of cmd pars
  1450 INX
  1460 LDA £&5F\Set verify cmd
  1470 STA &2F90,X\Save verify cmd
  1480 INX
  1490 LDA TRACK
  1500 STA &2F90,X\Save track addr
  1510 INX
  1520 LDA £0
  1530 STA &2F90,X\Save sector start
  1540 INX
  1550 LDA £&2A
  1560 STA &2F90,X\Save length/sector nos
  1570 INX
  1580 LDA £&FF
  1590 STA &2F90,X\Save dummy error code
  1600 RTS
  1610 .DCHAR
  1620 LDA TRACK
  1630 TAY\Save in Y
  1640 LDX £&FE\Set char counter
  1650 ROR A
  1660 ROR A
  1670 ROR A
  1680 ROR A
  1690 .CHAR2
  1700 AND £&0F\Mask top nibble
  1710 SEC\Set carry for subtraction
  1720 SBC £&0A\Separate letter/number
  1730 BCS TX1\Carry set=letter A-F
  1740 ADC £&3A\Convert no. to ASCII
  1750 BCS TX2
  1760 .TX1
  1770 ADC £&40\Convert letter to ASCII
  1780 .TX2
  1790 JSR OSASCI\Output to screen
  1800 INX\Another nibble?
```

```
>L.1810,
 1810 BEQ TX3\Jump if finished
 1820 TYA\Recover byte
 1830 JMP CHAR2
 1840 .TX3
 1850 RTS
 1860 ]
 1870 NEXT X
 1880 PRINT"Verifying Drive  ";DRI%;" - Please wait"
 1890 PRINT
 1900 CALL&3200
 1910 PRINT
 1915 IF ?DERR<>0THEN PRINT"Disk not formatted":GOTO1950
 1920 PRINT ?TCOUNT;" Track Disk":PRINT
 1930 PRINT"Drive ";DRI%;" verify complete"
 1940 PRINT ?VERR;" Verify errors"
 1950 END
```

This then completes the explanation of disk formatting and verification and with the information given, it should be possible to modify the routines, for example, formatting disks on the BBC Microcomputer to be compatible with other machine disk formats if required or for formatting 8" disk drives which have 77 tracks for use with the BBC Microcomputer.

Further details on the disk controller can be found by reference to the INTEL data sheet on the 8271 Floppy Disk Controller.

"WP" Word Handling Program

"WP" is an abbreviation for Word Processing and was the first text handling program written for the BBC Microcomputer. The original, called Text Line program was published in the Computer Users Club monthly journal during April 1982. The Computer Users Club produce software marketed as Good Company Software. Since then many books have been constructed using the program, all of which contain acknowledgements to its compatibility. The version contained herein is specifically written for use with the Epson type of printer (Model II or Model III) but it has been found that the program is readily adaptable to other makes of printer, since the adjustments usually involve changes to only three lines of the program. These adjustments will be discussed later.

The usefulness of this program as far as we are concerned lies in its handling of an array containing the text lines with regard to the storing and retrieval of this array onto either floppy disk or tape. An array can be thought of as a filing cabinet containing many drawers. Our cabinet has the name T$ and contains 61 drawers. We can place one line of text into each drawer.

Clearly a high volume of text saved as strings within the memory of the computer, together with the program that handles the array, would use a large amount of memory. To overcome this only one page of text at a time is constructed and the completed page is then saved on the disk for later use. The completed pages may be recalled at any time, sent out to a printer, viewed or amended as required.

By experience it has been noted that a page looks at its best when it contains approximately 58 lines of 65 characters per line. Each line of text as seen on the Visual Display Unit (VDU) begins with a number which is used for reference purposes only during construction of the page. Any line of text can be called by number into a position where it may be deleted or edited in a variety of ways, the new line being constructed always at one location known as the input line.

If for any reason you should manage to get into difficulties whilst using the program, press ESCAPE and type GOTO250 then press RETURN. This will direct you to the point in the program where it is awaiting the entry of your next command or line of text on the input line.

On running the program it begins by asking if you require instructions. In my own version a YES response to this question loads a built file, i.e. a file constructed using *BUILD "(fsp)", onto the screen memory and the file in effect is the operating instructions such as you are reading at this moment.

If you do not require the instructions simply press RETURN whereupon a numbered grid will be drawn at the bottom of the screen together with an abbreviated description of what each of the User Definable Function Keys will do if depressed. It is at this point that you are asked how long a line of text you require and the entry can be a number between 20 and 80.

We will assume for the moment that you enter 65. The actual length of line that you type in when entering text may differ from the length you have just specified. Where this difference is less than 7 characters the length of the line will be increased using the dot resolution capability of the Epson printer. In actual fact one single dot row where no needles from the print head are fired is used between each character contained on the line being printed. This has the effect of pushing the width of the line until it equals the 65 characters that we have specified and is called 'right hand justification'.

"WP" then functions as an electric typewriter. There are no restrictions regarding the type of characters that can be used on the line that you are entering. The user can copy other existing lines and words using the four arrowed cursor keys and the key as in normal screen editing. At the completion of each line entered the RETURN key places that line into the array. The position in the array, i.e. which drawer is being used, is held in an index marker called L%.

The area from the top of the screen down to the numbered grid is defined as a Scrolling Text Window. For users wishing to translate the program for machines not capable of providing a scrolling text window, there are ways round the problem insofar as the entire screen could be cleared and the numbered grid together with the associated function key descriptions reprinted at the bottom.

The Function Keys

"f0". This key calls the printer and prompts the user to enter a number of values to guide and control the printer. The first of these values determines how many copies of the text will be produced. If your text contains more than 32 lines, the program will generate an automatic Form Feed (FF) provided that you have requested more than one copy.

The second prompt asks if you require a tabulation setting. This is not to be confused with normal tabulation which can be arranged by inserting Embedded Commands inside the text lines. The tabulation referred to here really pushes the start of the left hand margin of all lines to a pre-determined position according to the number entered.

The third prompt asks if you require right hand justification. Justification is only possible where the line length is greater than 42 characters. All lines entered whose length is within 7 characters of the chosen line length will be justified at the right hand side.

Embedded Command Codes

Command codes can be offered inside curly brackets as {XX} where the value of {XX} is a decimal ASCII value listed in Table V of the Epson Handbook and on Table VI at the back of this book. Where ESC (Escape) is required before the actual command number it will be generated automatically by the program, i.e. ESC 69 will tell the printer to embolden the text. This is offered in the data line as {69}.

User Definable Key f1

Where tape filing is required as opposed to disk, f1 conditions the computer for tape to be the currently selected filing system. A file name 'Page X' where 'X' is an incrementing number is assumed, but you are offered the option of saving the page under any name that you specify. At the time of specifying the name you should not specify the number for you will be asked the number after entering the name. The reason for this is to allow, in the case of a book being written, for each page generated to be saved as Page 1, Page 2 etc. whilst at the same time allowing Table I, Table II etc. to be generated in between the pages as required.

f1 is also used to recall previously saved pages of text from a tape filing system. When disks are being used a catalog showing the pages is presented on the screen in order to remind you of the file names previously used. This of course is not possible, or at least is possible but would be long-winded, when tape filing is the currently selected system, and it is far easier to keep a record elsewhere as to which pages are contained on that particular cassette.

User Definable Key f2

The key f2 is used to locate the last available line number for text entry. Imagine for a moment that a small amount of text had been entered and that a number of blank lines had been created by pressing RETURN without any text entry. Line numbers are thus in this way incremented to leave a space. Let us say the space is required to contain a drawing. At this point, whilst you are about to enter a paragraph that would appear below the drawing, you remember additional material that you would like to add to the original paragraph above the drawing. It is possible to insert these additional lines using another key which will be discussed later, but you are able to move back to the original paragraph using f2. In fact this brings you back to the first empty line under the text.

User Definable Key f3

f3 is designed to allow you to preview existing text. It presents the text in the scrolling window from line 1 onwards in page mode, each screenful consisting of 8 lines which are updated to the next 8 when the space bar is depressed. At the end of the text the program returns to the condition awaiting your next command or further text.

User Definable Key f4

Text can be altered using this key. The prompt asks you which line requires alteration and in response to a line number, that line is presented immediately above the input line which allows the use of the normal BBC Computer edit facilities to reprint the line on the input line together with whatever adjustments are necessary.

User Definable Key f5

f5 when pressed will centre the last previously entered line. Let us assume for the moment that a heading is required in underscored emboldened face, to be placed in the center of the text. This would be achieved as follows:

The line would start with: { 45 } 001

The{45} followed by 1 tells the printer to turn on the underline.

Next we insert {69} which tells the printer to enter emboldened mode. In both the above cases an escape control code would have been sent preceding the actual command code. We now enter the text and afterwards we enter {70} which equals 'finished with emboldening' followed by { 45} 000 which means 'finished with underline'. The whole line is shown below:

{45} 001 {67} The Text {70}{45} 000

The line is then entered by pressing RETURN. Next it is centered by pressing f5.

User Definable Key f6

When a new page is required, after the last page has been saved on the filing system f6 is pressed and has the effect of clearing existing text from the array starting again at line 1.

User Definable Key f7

This command is used to delete whole lines. The prompt which appears on the screen requires an entry of the line number to be deleted. Once deleted all other lines in the array are moved up one to compensate for the gap created.

User Definable Key f8

Insertion of the last entry line into any other line position is possible using f8 i.e. if a line of text is entered and f8 pressed a prompt appears asking 'which line?'. If 16 is input as the line number then the line will be inserted at line 16 and all lines below 16 including the previous occupant of line 16 will be moved down one to compensate. Whole paragraphs can be inserted by typing them in one line at a time and inserting in the manner described above.

User Definable Key f9

The disk filing system is called and handled by f9. The catalog of file names is shown before your choice of page is entered for loading and also shown after your page has been saved in order that you can ensure that your text is safely filed.

Where a code appears as ESC X+n or ESC X+n1+n2 the value for 'n' or n2 can be treated as three digit decimal numbers placed after the brackets (without spaces). For example on an Epson MX80 F/T III ESC S+(n)D [Superscript]. one would enter {83}000 to set superscript or {83}001 for subscripts. In this manner every aspect of printer control can be obtained from within the text line.

Dot Graphics

The three digit numbers that follow the brackets will produce all graphics for that line. The numbers should be ended by '}}}' e.g.

{75}012 000 004 010 026 058 103 231 103 058 026 010 004 }}}

will produce (note spaces are for clarity only): ◆

The program is primarily intended for use with parallel printer interfaces but there is no reason why it should not work equally as well with serial printer interfaces provided that the appropriate output and baud rate are selected, which can be achieved by adding one line to the program.

Serial printer is called using *FX5,2 and once selected requires that the baud rate to match the printer's requirement is also entered. The baud rate selection codes are as follows:

*FX8,8	19200 baud
*FX8,7	9600 baud
*FX8,6	4800 baud
*FX8,5	2400 baud
*FX8,4	1200 baud
*FX8,3	300 baud
*FX8,2	150 baud
*FX8,1	75 baud

On certain printers, internal switches inside the printer arrange for the automatic generation of line feed and carriage return signals. It may well be that these switches within your printer are set to the conditions which, in conjunction with the program, causes double line feeds. To overcome this some experimentation with the lines 110 and 790 will be necessary.

In some cases the value *FX6,0 (known as a printer ignore character) would require changing to *FX5,1. If the printer requires the receive baud rate to be different from the transmit baud rate, receive baud rate are set by *FX7,X as opposed to *FX8,X listed above where X can be 1-8.

In extreme cases the user can define his own printer output routines and place the address where his routine lies to indirect via &0222 which then becomes an indirection vector (see operating system filing commands), which enables the printer output routine to be called with *FX5,3, but in general it has never been necessary to use this technique.

Where Daisy Wheel printers are used it should be noted that the underscore uses {25} before and after the words to be underscored as opposed to the Epson {45} n.

Hints on Conversion

In converting for other computers line 30 could be ignored. At line 190 PROCOption you would use GOSUB 1980 with the return placed at 2110. Wherever the BBC machine says PROCXX you will find further down the listing Def ProcXXX which is the point that gosubs are attacted to, the nearest endproc after that point being the return. Within the subroutines if you have not got user defined keys, enter the lines as [X], X being a letter as shown in lines 2010-2100. You will be entering the identifier to call tape, printer etc.

Line 150 prints a mini logo across the screen to physically separate the text window from the displayed prompts. You can simply draw a line across the screen to serve this purpose. Line 200 defines the scrolling window. If this is not possible on your machine simply arrange to scroll the whole screen and reprint the options and the grid.

Line 200 VDU 15 means leave page mode and may be omitted. Line 280 calls two procedures to be executed within a loop. ProcNo can be found at 1910-1940. Line 1920 states @%=&00000902: this arranges for numbers to be printed in a format that contains only two digits. You can simulate on most machines using a PRINT USING statement. Line 1930 restores normal number handling before returning from the subroutines. Line 1950 prints out the lines of text from the array on the screen relevant to the current line number.

The text you enter is accepted at line 350. The BBC machine uses INPUT LINE which allows quotation marks and any other information without limitation to be entered. On most other machines the accidental entry of " " within strings would give rise to a type mismatched error.

To eliminate this possibility the lines could be constructed as follows:

```
350   I=INKEY(0)
351   IF I = 35 THEN 350
352   IF I = -1 THEN 350
353   IF I = 13 THEN 360
354   IF I = 127 THEN (Proc. to deduct CHR$)
355   U$ = U$ + CHR$(I)
356   GOTO 350
```

WORDPRO PROGRAM

```
>L.10,450
   10 REM *(C) 1982 TONY LATHAM *
   20  REM * THE COMPUTER USERS CLUB *
   30 U$=STRING$(81,"?"):U$=""
   40 UN$=STRING$(1,"?"):UN$=""
   50 C%=1 :F%=0
   60 *TV0,1
   70 MODE3
   80 CLEAR:DIMT$(61)
   90 CO%=0:F2%=0
  100 CLS
  110 *FX6,0
  120 VDU31,0,22
  130 G%=10:L%=0
  140 REPEAT
  150    PRINT"----¦---";G%;
  160    G%=G%+10
  170    UNTILG%>80
  180 L%=L%+1
  190 PROCOptions
  200 VDU15;28,0,19,79,1
  210 VDU31,0,18
  220 INPUT"No of CHAR per line . DEFAULT 80 ",W%
  230 IFW%>80ORW%<1THENW%=80
  240 PRINT;"(PAGE = 60 X ";W%;" LINES/CHAR.)"
  250 REM
  260 IF L%<8 THEN C%=0 ELSE C%=L%-7
  270 FORLP= C% TO L%
  280    PRINTLP
  290    PRINTT$(LP)
  300    NEXTLP
  310 PRINT"ENTER TEXT OR OPTION"
  320 R%=L%
  330 PROCNO
  340 U$="":CO%=0
  350 REPEAT
  360    UN$=GET$
  370    U$=U$+UN$
  380    PRINTUN$;
  390    IFUN$="{"THENF2%=1
  400    IFF2%=1 CO%=CO%+1
  410    IFUN$=CHR$127 PROCDEL
  420    IFUN$="}"THENF2%=0
  430    IFLEN(U$)-CO%=W%-7 SOUND1,-12,100,5
  440    UNTILUN$=CHR$13 OR LEN(U$)-CO%=W%
  450 IFUN$=CHR$13THEN U$=MID$(U$,1,LEN(U$)-1)
```

```
>L.460.,900
  460 C1$=LEFT$(U$,1)
  470 C2$=MID$(U$,4,1)
  480 IFC1$="[" AND C2$="]" U$=MID$(U$,2,2):G%=VAL(U$)ELSEG%=1
  490 IFG%<0 OR G%>11THEN350
  500 ONG%GOTO510,900,940,970,1080,1180,70,2380,2440,2120,570
  510 T$(L%)=U$
  520 IFT%>0 L%=T%:T%=0:GOTO250
  530 IFL%>59 L=60:PROCFULL:GOTO460
  540 L%=L%+1
  550 PRINT
  560 GOTO320
  570 REMPRINTER
  580 PQ=0
  590 PRINT
  600 INPUT"HOW MANY COPIES",QU
  610 INPUT"INPUT TAB-DEFAULT NONE",TB
  620 IFW%>42 INPUT"SET 1=JUSTIFY,DEFAULT 'NOT'",K2 ELSEK2=0
  630 PRINT
  640 INPUT"POSITION PAPER,THEN RETURN",QME$
  650 VDU2
  660 FOR R=1 TO (L%-1)
  670   U$=T$(R)
  680   S=LEN(U$)
  690   F1=0:F2=0:JF=0
  700   IFTB>60 VDU1,15;:JF=1
  710   IFTB>0 VDU1,27;1,68;1,(TB);1,0;1,137;
  720   IFK2=0THEN740
  730   J%=W%-S:IFJ%<8 AND J%>0 PROCJUST:GOTO680
  740   FORLP=1TOS
  750     CS$=MID$(U$,LP,1):CD$=MID$(U$,(LP+3),1)
  760     CE$=MID$(U$,(LP+1),1)
  770     IFCS$="{" AND CD$="}" PROCFACE:GOTO800
  780       IFCS$="]" AND CE$="[" LP=LP+1:VDU1,27;1,K1;
                1,1;1,0;1,0;:GOTO800
  790     PRINTCS$;
  800     NEXTLP
  810   VDU13:VDU10
  820   NEXTR
  830 GAP=65-L%
  840 PQ=PQ+1
  850 VDU3
  860 PRINT:PRINT"PAGE ";C%;" COPIES= ";PQ
  870 IF NOT (QU=PQ)AND(GAP>30)THEN640
  880 IF NOT (QU=PQ)AND(GAP<31)THEN VDU1,12:VDU3:GOTO650
  890 GOTO250
  900 *TAPE
```

```
>L.910,1350
  910 INPUTTAB(7),"DO YOU WISH TO LOAD",QU$
  920 IF LEFT$(QU$,1)="Y"THENPROCFETCH:GOTO250
  930 PROCDITCH:GOTO250
  940 REM
  950 IFT$(L%)=""THENL%=L%-1:GOTO950
  960 L%=L%+1:GOTO250
  970 REM
  980 R%=0:PRINT
  990 N=INT((L%+8)/9)
 1000 FORC=1TON
 1010    FORK=1TO8
 1020      R%=R%+1
 1030      PROCNO:PROCLINE
 1040      NEXTK
 1050    PRINT"KEY=CONTINUE":QU$=GET$
 1060    NEXTC
 1070 GOTO250
 1080 REM
 1090 INPUT"WHICH LINE",QU
 1100 G%=0
 1110 IFQU>8THENG%=QU-8
 1120 FOR R%=G% TO QU
 1130    PROCNO
 1140    PROCLINE
 1150    NEXTR%
 1160 T%=L%:L%=QU
 1170 GOTO320
 1180 REM
 1190 QU=L%-1
 1200 S=LEN(T$(QU))
 1210 IFS<3THEN T$(QU)="   "+T$(QU)
 1220 I=INSTR(T$(QU),"{14}")
 1230 IFI=0THEN1240ELSE1260
 1240 VA=INT(W%-S)/2
 1250 GOTO1290
 1260 S=INT(S-8)
 1270 VA=INT((W%/2)-S)
 1280 IFS>38THENS=W%:GOTO1240
 1290 U$=T$(QU)
 1300 FOR R=1 TO VA
 1310    U$=" "+U$
 1320    NEXTR
 1330 T$(QU)=U$
 1340 GOTO250
 1350 DEFPROCFETCH
```

```
>L.1360,1800
 1360 IFF%>0 THEN F%=0 : *.
 1370 PRINT"INSERT DATA TAPE/DISC"
 1375 PRINT"FILENAME = PAGE";C%
 1380 PRINT:INPUT"DO YOU WANT A SPECIAL FILE",DU$
 1390 IFDU$="YES"ORDU$="Y"THENPROCCHANGE:GOTO1420
 1400 INPUT"WHICH PAGE NUMBER",QU%
 1410 A$="PAGE"+STR$(QU%)
 1420 ONERRORGOTO1520
 1430 B=OPENIN(A$)
 1440 L%=1
 1450 REPEAT
 1460    INPUT£B,T$(L%)
 1470    L%=L%+1
 1480    UNTIL EOF£B
 1490 CLOSE£B
 1500 L%=L%-1
 1510 ENDPROC
 1520 REPORT
 1530 PRINT"SORRY-ERROR"
 1540 IFERR=17THENEND
 1550 GOTO330
 1560 DEFPROCDITCH
 1570 A$="PAGE"+STR$(C%)
 1580 PRINT"THIS FILENAME IS"
 1590 PRINT
 1600 PRINTTAB(6),A$
 1610 PRINT
 1620 INPUT"DO YOU WISH TO CHANGE THIS",QU$
 1630 A$="PAGE"+STR$(C%)
 1640 IFLEFT$(QU$,1)="Y"THENPROCCHANGE
 1650 PRINT"INSERT DATA DISK(TAPE SET FOR RECORD)"
 1660 INPUT"ENTER WHEN READY",G%
 1670 ONERRORGOTO1770
 1680 B=OPENOUT(A$)
 1690 FORR=1TOL%
 1700    PRINT£B,T$(R)
 1710    NEXTR
 1720 CLOSE£B
 1730 C%=C%+1
 1735  IF F%=0 THEN 1750
 1740 *.
 1750 INPUT"KEY = CONTINUE"G%
 1760 ENDPROC
 1770 REPORT
 1780 PRINT"ERROR"
 1790 IFERR=17THENEND
 1800 GOTO250
```

WORDPRO PROGRAM

```
>L.1010,810,2250
 1810 DEFPROCCHANGE
 1820 INPUT"WHAT NAME",D$
 1830 INPUT"WHAT NUMBER",C%
 1840 A$=D$+STR$(C%)
 1850 ENDPROC
 1860 DEFPROCFULL
 1870 PRINT'"PAGE FULL,SAVE TEXT"
 1880 PRINT"OR ENTER OPTION"
 1890 INPUTU$:IFLEFT$(U$,1)<>"["THENL%=L%+1:GOTO1890
 1900 ENDPROC
 1910 DEFPROCNO
 1920 VDU15:@%=&00000902
 1930 PRINTR%:@%=2570
 1940 ENDPROC
 1950 DEFPROCLINE
 1960 PRINTT$(R%)
 1970 ENDPROC
 1980 DEFPROCOptions
 1990   PRINT TAB(8);"F0= PRINTER.   F1= TAPE.
              F2= LAST LINE.   F3= READ.   F4= ALTER."
 2000   PRINT TAB(8);"F5= CENTRE.    F6= NEW PAGE.
              F7= DELETE.      F8= INSERT.F9= DISC."
 2010 *KEY0[11]¦M
 2020 *KEY1[02]¦M
 2030 *KEY2[03]¦M
 2040 *KEY3[04]¦M
 2050 *KEY4[05]¦M
 2060 *KEY5[06]¦M
 2070 *KEY6[07]¦M
 2080 *KEY7[08]¦M
 2090 *KEY8[09]¦M
 2100 *KEY9[10]¦M
 2110 ENDPROC
 2120 *DISK
 2130 INPUT"WHICH DRIVE FOR DATA ",G%
 2140 IF G%=3 THEN *DRIVE3
 2150 IF G%=2 THEN *DRIVE2
 2160 IF G%=1 THEN *DRIVE1
 2165 IF G%=0 THEN *DRIVE0
 2170 *DIR$
 2180 T$(L%)=""
 2190 F%=1
 2200 GOTO910
 2210 DEFPROCFACE
 2220 LP=LP+1
 2230 CS$=MID$(U$,LP,2):GOTO2260
 2240 LP=LP+3
 2250 CS$=MID$(U$,LP,3)
```

```
>L.2260,2700
 2260 CS=VAL(CS$)
 2270 IFF2=1 AND CS$="}}}"THEN F2=0:GOTO2370
 2280 IFF2=1THEN2350
 2290 IFF1=1THENF1=0:GOTO2350
 2300 IFCS>21THENVDU1,27;
 2310 IFCS=45 ORCS=51 OR CS>65THENF1=1
 2320 IFCS=69 OR CS=70 OR CS=71 ORCS=72 OR CS=84 THENF1=0
 2330 IFCS=15THENJF=1
 2340 IFCS=18THENJF=0
 2350 VDU1,(CS);
 2360 IFF1=1 OR F2=1THEN2240
 2370 LP=LP+2:ENDPROC
 2380 INPUT"WHICH LINE ",QU
 2390 FORLP=QU TOL%
 2400    T$(LP)=T$((LP+1))
 2410    NEXTLP
 2420 L%=L%-1
 2430 GOTO250
 2440 INPUT"WHICH LINE ",QU
 2450 M%=L%+1
 2460 FORLP=L%TO(QU+1)STEP-1
 2470    T$(LP)=T$(LP-1)
 2480    NEXTLP
 2490 T$(LP)=T$(L%)
 2500 T$(L%)=""
 2510 GOTO250
 2520 DEFPROCJUST
 2530 PT%=1:V$="":BL%=S:FG=0
 2540 LM%=(J%*6)
 2550 IFJF>0 K1=75ELSEK1=76
 2560 FOR MR%=1 TO LM%
 2570    CS$=MID$(U$,PT%,1)
 2580    IFCS$="{"THENFG=7
 2590    IFFG>0THENFG=FG-1
 2600    V$=V$+CS$
 2610    IFFG=0THENV$=V$+"}{"
 2620    PT%=PT%+1:BL%=BL%-1
 2630    NEXTMR%
 2640 U$=V$+RIGHT$(U$,BL%)
 2650 ENDPROC
 2660 DEFPROCDEL
 2670 U$=MID$(U$,1,LEN(U$)-2)
 2680 IFCO%<>0ANDF2%=1 CO%=CO%-2
 2690 ENDPROC
```

TABLE 7.1

MAJOR CONTROL CODES			
Control Code	Hex.	Dec.	Function
NUL	00	0	NULL. Ends tab setting. Follows ESC B, ESC C and ESC D.
BEL	07	7	BELL. Sounds buzzer for about 0.3 second.
BS	08	8	Backspace. The data stored in the buffer is printed and the buffer point is decremented by 1.
DEL	7F	127	Clears the last data in the print buffer.
HT	09	9	Horizontal Tabulation.
LF	0A	10	Line Feed.
VT	0B	11	Vertical Tabulation.
FF	0C	12	Form Feed. Advances paper to next Top of Form.
CR	0D	13	Carriage Return.
SO	0E	14	Shift Out. Turns on the enlarged character printing mode.
SI	0F	15	Shift In. Turns on the condensed character printing mode.

TABLE 7.1 - MAJOR CONTROL CODES

Control Code	Hex.	Dec.	Function
DC2	12	18	Turns off the condensed character printing mode.
DC4	14	20	Turns off the enlarged character printing mode.
ESC	1B	27	Escape. ASCII code for Escape. Precedes numbers and alphabets.
ESC 0	30	48	Sets a line spacing to 8 lines per inch.
ESC 1	31	49	Sets a line spacing to 7/72".
ESC 2	32	50	Sets a line spacing to 6 lines per inch.
ESC 3	33	51	Sets a line spacing to n/216".
ESC 8	38	56	Deselects paper end detector.
ESC 9	39	57	Selects paper end detector.
ESC A	41	65	Sets a line spacing between a range from 1/72" to 85/72".
ESC B	42	66	Sets VT up to 8 positions.
ESC C	43	67	Sets form length.
ESC D	44	68	Sets HT up to 12 positions.
ESC E	45	69	Turns on the emphasized character printing mode.
ESC F	46	70	Turns off the emphasized character printing mode.
ESC G	47	71	Turns on the double character printing mode.

TABLE 7.1 - MAJOR CONTROL CODES

Control	Hex.	Dec.	Function
ESC H	48	72	Turns off the double character printing mode.
ESC J	4A	74	Sets a line spacing to n/216"
ESC K	4B	75	Turns on the normal density bit image mode.
ESC L	4C	76	Turns on the dual density bit image mode.
ESC N	4E	78	Set skip-over perforation.
ESC O	4F	79	Releases skip-over perforation.
ESC Q	51	81	Sets a column length.
ESC R	52	82	Selects an international character set from among 8 languages.
ESC S	53	83	Turns on the superscript/subscript mode.
ESC T	54	84	Turns off the superscript/subscript mode.
ESC U	55	85	Starts or ends Unidirectional printing.
ESC W	57	87	Turns on or off the enlarged character printing mode.
ESC -	2D	45	Turns on or off the underlined printing mode.
ESC @	40	64	Initializes Printer.

8 Technical Details

Without considering one particular make of disk drive unit it is difficult to give absolute technical specifications. However, the values given in this chapter relate to a typical drive.

The functional requirements of the unit are listed below and we will discuss each in turn. It is not necessary for the layman to understand this chapter, but it is included for the benefit of technically minded users desiring to interface their own particular drive.

(a) Interpret and generate control signals;
(b) locate the desired track by moving the read/write head;
(c) read and write the data;
(d) control the motor speed;
(e) sense the environment;

(a) Control Signals

The hardware which controls the disk can be considered as two inter-related halves, one of which is inside the BBC Computer and the other is mounted onto the disk drive chassis. The two are connected by a flat ribbon cable which has 34 wires along which data and control signals are interchanged.

Fig. 8.1 shows a schematic diagram of the computer end of the hardware.

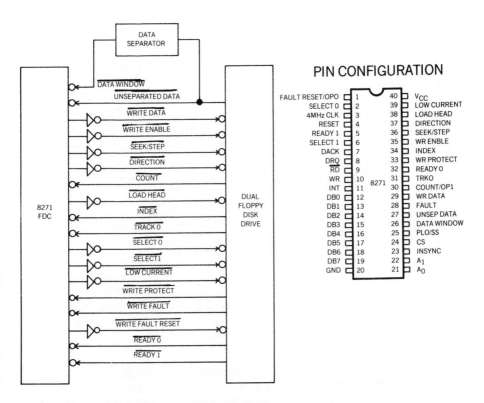

Fig. 8.1 Connections to the Disk Controller

The main integrated circuit involved is an INTEL 8271 Programmable Floppy Disk Controller (FDC) which is itself powerful enough to minimize both the hardware and software requirements.

The storage system used is comparable with the IBM 3740 soft sectored format and the chip is powered from a single +5 V supply.

Input/Output Line Terminations

The FDD (Floppy Disk Drive) provides the capability by terminating the following lines through a 150 ohm resistor pack installed in a dip socket on the circuit board (see Fig. 8.2).

1.	Motor on	4.	Write data
2.	Direction select	5.	Write gate
3.	Step	6.	Drive select (1 through 4).

The drive units are normally shipped from the factory with the resistor pack installed. These lines must be terminated for proper operation.

In a multiple drive configuration, only the last FDD in the configuration is to be terminated. All other FDDs on the interface must have the resistor pack removed. In addition, the program-shunt-module-position 'MX' must be open.

External termination may be used, in which case the host equipment may provide the termination beyond the last FDD. The lines must be terminated to +5 VDC through a 150 ohm 1/4 watt resistor, and the typical total line length should not exceed 10 feet (3.05 m).

Where a switch option card is fitted to drive 0 to enable the selection of either 80 or 40 track modes, the resistor pack must be in drive 0, otherwise, when the system is switched to the 40 track mode the line would not be loaded. An unloaded line gives rise to error 18 (drive fault).

Link Selection

Selection of drive 0 or drive 1 by the computer utilizes 2 lines called select lines, which can be seen in Fig. 8.1. At the drive end, these two lines have to be decoded and the program shunt module is responsible for part of the decode.

When a drive unit arrives as new from the factory, all the links are intact on the small dual-in-line (DIL) plug which fits into the socket shown in Fig. 8.2. The links are broken by a pointed object to configure the drive to be either 0 or 1 according to its intended position inside the chassis.

Fig. 8.2 inset shows which combinations of links remain intact for most makes of drive. On a Teac however, the link corresponding to the symbol 'X' (multiplex OPT(MX)) also needs to be left intact on both drives of a double drive unit. If this is not done, the drive motors will run in response to *. but no data transfer can occur.

The PCB inside the BBC Microcomputer has a number of removable links (jumpers) which affect disk handling as outlined below.

Option select link S4 EAST	=	Select $5\frac{1}{4}$ inch(13.3cm)
WEST	=	Select 8 inch(20.3cm)
Option select link S7 EAST	=	Apply +0 V to pin 30 of disk controller (IC78)
WEST	=	Apply +5 V to pin 30
Option select link S8 Closed	=	Link disk head load signal to PL9
Open	=	Isolate disk head load signal from PL8
Option select link S9 Closed	=	Disable disk NMI (NMI = non maskable interrupt)
Open	=	Enable disk NMI

Note: I/C 78 should not be fitted with S9 closed. Due to PCB fault on early computers (PCB issue 1 and issue 2) issue 3 boards have this link as a track on the component side of the board, which must be cut when NMI (non maskable interrupts) from the disk are required.

Option Link S10   WEST   = $5\frac{1}{4}$ inch(13.3cm)
                          EAST   = 8 inch(20.3cm)

On the keyboard, beneath the right hand SHIFT key is a double row of holes which can contain wire links which affect the seek time for different makes of drive unit. The links are counted from left to right and should be arranged according to Table 8.1.

For example, Tandon disk drives with 4 ms access require both links made. Tandon and Shugart disk drives with 6 ms access require 3 made, 4 unmade.

TABLE 8.1 - LINK SETTINGS FOR VARIOUS DRIVE TYPES

Links								Affects	Timing
1	2	3	4	5	6	7	8	Normal operation	
								Olivetti, CDC, Shugart	
		X	X					Tandon	4 ms
		X						Tandon, Shugart	6 ms
			X					MPI	
				X				Break auto start action (without shift) 5 off is shift held	

Switches 1 and 2 are not used (unassigned).
Switches 6, 7, 8 set the start up mode after BREAK. All three links made gives Mode 0 then logically unmaking the switch to dictate the mode number, e.g.

                6   7   8
                M   M   U   =   Mode 1

where M is made and U is unmade.

Performance Characteristics

The equipment specifications for typical FDD are as follows:

	Single density
Capacity	
Unformatted	
Per disk	125 kbytes
Per track	3125 bytes
Formatted (16 sectors, 128/256 bytes)	
Per disk	81.92 kbytes
Per track	2048 bytes
Code	FM
Transfer rate	125 kbits /s
Average latency	100 ms
Seek time	
Track to track	20 ms
Average	275 ms
Setting time	15 ms
Head load time	50 ms
Media	hard/soft sector
Rotational speed	300 r/min
Track density	48 TPI
Flux reversal density (track 39)	5537 FRI
Number of tracks	40
Inner recorded radius	1.437 inch(36.5 mm)
Outer recorded radius	2.250 inch(57.2 mm)

Double Density

Capacity	
Unformatted	
Per disk	250 kbytes
Per track	6250 bytes
Formatted (16 sectors, 128/256 bytes)	
Per disk	163.84 kbytes
Per track	4096 bytes
Code	MFM
Transfer rate	250 kbits /s
Average latency	100 ms
Seek time	
Track to track	20 ms
Average	275 ms
Setting time	15 ms
Head load time	50 ms
Media	hard/soft sector
Rotational speed	300 r/min
Track density	48 TPI
Flux reversal density (track 39)	5537 FRI
Number of tracks	40
Inner recorded radius	1.437 inch(36.5 mm)
Outer recorded radius	2.250 inch(57.2 mm)

It should be noted that the BBC Computer disk hardware and software (DFS) does not support double density. However it is possible that changes could come about in the fullness of time which will allow this method of storage. When double density is used the transfer rate of the information and the volume of storage is doubled. Double density packs the information onto tracks that are so close together that temperature changes affecting the expansion and contraction of the disk can give rise to read/write errors.

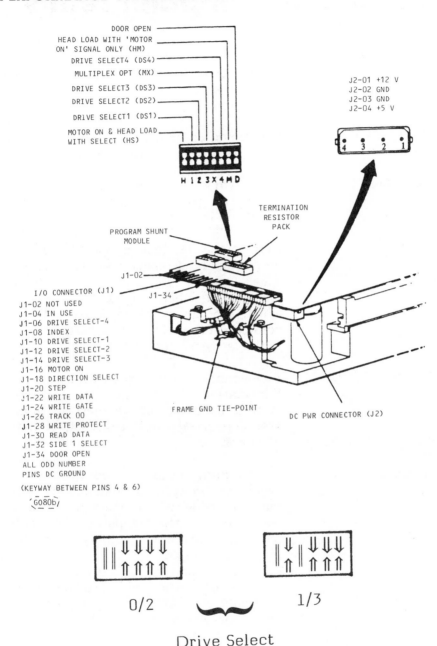

DOOR OPEN

HEAD LOAD WITH 'MOTOR
ON' SIGNAL ONLY (HM)

DRIVE SELECT4 (DS4)

MULTIPLEX OPT (MX)

DRIVE SELECT3 (DS3)

DRIVE SELECT2 (DS2)

DRIVE SELECT1 (DS1)

MOTOR ON & HEAD LOAD
WITH SELECT (HS)

H 1 2 3 X 4 M D

J2-01 +12 V
J2-02 GND
J2-03 GND
J2-04 +5 V

4 3 2 1

TERMINATION
RESISTOR
PACK

PROGRAM SHUNT
MODULE

J1-02

J1-34

I/O CONNECTOR (J1)

J1-02 NOT USED
J1-04 IN USE
J1-06 DRIVE SELECT-4
J1-08 INDEX
J1-10 DRIVE SELECT-1
J1-12 DRIVE SELECT-2
J1-14 DRIVE SELECT-3
J1-16 MOTOR ON
J1-18 DIRECTION SELECT
J1-20 STEP
J1-22 WRITE DATA
J1-24 WRITE GATE
J1-26 TRACK 00
J1-28 WRITE PROTECT
J1-30 READ DATA
J1-32 SIDE 1 SELECT
J1-34 DOOR OPEN
ALL ODD NUMBER
PINS DC GROUND

(KEYWAY BETWEEN PINS 4 & 6)

G080b

FRAME GND TIE-POINT

DC PWR CONNECTOR (J2)

0/2

1/3

Drive Select

Fig. 8.2 Typical 1.0 Interface (JI), DC Power (J2), and Resistor

Glossary of Computer Terms

ACCUMULATOR

The area inside a microprocessor in which computations take place and where the results of such computations are stored.

ALPHANUMERIC

Pertaining to alphabetic characters and numbers mixed, i.e. as a keyboard.

AMPERSAND

The symbol '&' used by the BBC Computer to mean that the number following is in Hexadecimal.

ARRAY

Arrays can be looked upon as multi-dimensional variables. An area is put aside using a DIM statement (Dimension) such as DIM test$(4,10) which would set aside 4 rows of 10 columns for anything you care to save in this array called test$.

ASCII

American Standard Code for Information Interchange. An encoding system used on alphanumerics, which are converted into seven-bit binary numbers.

ASSEMBLER

A program used to convert other programs written in mnemonics into machine code where machine code is understood by the computer. Assembly language runs more quickly than high level languages. It consists of commands such as SBC (subtract) and ADC (add). The end product of an assembly is a set of binary instructions known as an object code listing which, when run as a program, is several hundred times faster than BASIC.

BASIC	An acronym (alternate abbreviated name) meaning Beginners All-purpose Symbolic Instruction Code. Although this system has certain limitations it is very easy to learn since the commands plus statements resemble ordinary English.
BAUD	Approximately one bit per second, a measure of the rate of transfer of information, named after Baudot, an engineer.
BBC COMPUTER	The name given to a microcomputer manufactured by Acorn Computers Ltd.
BIT	BInary digiT, an abbreviation. A bit is the smallest unit of information recognizable by a computer.
BLANK	Refers to a disk not yet formatted. Contains no information.
BOOT	Taken from the expression 'lifting oneself with the bootstraps', Boot is taken to mean forced into a particular condition.
BREAK	(BREAK key) Used on the BBC Computer to reset start-up conditions. Causes what is known as a cold-start condition where data or programs can be lost. OLD retains a program providing that no other matter is entered at the keyboard between BREAK and OLD.
BUBBLE MEMORY	A method of storing data using localized pockets of magnetism inside a semiconductor.

BUFFER

A block of Random Access Memory used as a temporary store for incoming information.

BYTE

Usually taken as eight binary digits and also known as one binary word.

CATALOG

The list of programs contained on one disk surface.

CHAIN

The act of loading a program from disk or tape then executing the program.

CLOCK

A crystal controlled timing device within the computer that is used to synchronize all operations.

CODES

A system of letters or symbols enabling brief communication where the letters or symbols represent binary notation for use by the computer.

COMPLEMENT

A number derived from another by logical subtraction.

COMPUTER

A device containing integrated circuits with three main capabilities (1) to accept data, (2) to solve problems, and (3) to output results.

CPU

Central Processing Unit. An area contained within a micro chip in which instructions are interpreted and calculations performed.

DATA

Information in digital form.

DEFAULT

Refers to the condition assumed in the absence of instructions to the computer.

DFS	Disk File System - a program in ROM designed to handle communication with the disk drive controlled hardware.
DIGITAL	Derived originally from the word digit representing a finger or toe. It means in this context a counting system (binary) represented by 1's or 0's.
DISK/DISC	A circular plastic base coated with a magnetically sensitized layer, used for storing information.
DISK CONTROLLER	A semiconductor device which handles the communication between the disk drive and the microcomputer.
DISK DRIVE	An electro-mechanical device used to store and retrieve information from a disk.
DISPLACEMENT	A value indicating memory address relative to a pre-set pointer. The range is usually limited to +128 -127.
DOUBLE DENSITY	A technique which allows twice the number of sectors to be stored on a disk surface. The BBC computer hardware and software does not support double density.
DOUBLE TRACKING	Often used to mean 80 track disk drives or disks. 80 track disks are those which have a track density of 96 tpi (tracks per inch).
DROP INS	Spurious bits or bytes written onto the disk as a result of power surges or spikes.

DROP OUTS   Spurious bits or bytes deleted as a result of power surges or spikes.

ECONET   A method of connecting several computers into one file serving unit.

EMBEDDED COMMANDS   Commands included in a data block which are identified by the receiving device and serve to invoke special effects, i.e. turn on a printer's underscore.

EPROM   Eraseable Programmable Read Only Memory. Unlike ROM these devices can be reset by ultra-violet light and then re-programmed. Information is thus retained even when the power supply is disconnected.

EXECUTION ADDRESS   The address in memory representing the start of a numbered sequence of instructions.

FIELD   An area within a record of stored information.

FILE   A systematic arrangement of related items of information.

FILE HANDLE   Channel number allocated to an open file.

FILENAME   The name assigned to a file which is recorded on the disk or tape catalog. A filename, together with a drive number and directory letter, becomes a file specification.

FLAG   A memory area set to a pre-set logic state, to indicate a logical condition.

FLOPPY

See disk.

FLYING HEIGHT

The distance that the head assumes relative to a hard disk. This gap is maintained due to air pressure created by the aerodynamic shape of the head.

FORMAT

To arrange data on a magnetic medium in compliance with the requirements of the computers input devices.

FORTH

A language invented during 1970 by Charles Moore using an IBM 1400. The original conception of the name was FOURTH Generation Computer Language. The language is mainly used where speed and 'real time' problems are involved.

FORTRAN

An acronym meaning FORmula TRANslation. A high level language orientated towards problem interpretation, used mainly for maths and science purposes.

FREQUENCY
MODULATION

A method of transferring information as a continuous train of pulses, one pulse representing 0 and two pulses representing a logic 1.

HARDWARE

The physical components of a computer system.

HEAD

Part of a disk drive unit. The head is a magnetic device used to record and read back data onto a disk.

HEADCRASH

Describes the action of the head of a hard disk system fouling the disk surface, usually due to disruption of airflow caused by pollutants.

HEXADECIMAL (HEX)

A numbering system whose base is 16. In a decimal system, consider a units column that can be incremented from 0-9 and at the 10th count a new column is created containing a 1 on the left of the original unit column. With a base of 16, a new column is created after the 16th unit and since we only have numbers representing 0-9, alternate symbols are used for 10 to 15, after which a new column is created as for decimal systems. The symbols chosen are A to F, thus numbers such as 2FB1 are created.

HUB

The central hole sometimes surrounded by a hub ring (strengthener) on a disk. This is the area used by the drive spindle to centralize and grip a floppy disk.

IBM

The registered trading name of International Business Machines Ltd., the firm who created the IBM3740 format used by the (BBC) Disk File System.

IMPULSE

See Pulse.

INDEX HOLE   Situated on a floppy disk, this hole is used to optically detect the start of each track.

INPUT BUFFER   An area of Random Access Memory used to store temporarily the information arriving from the keyboard, tape recorder, disk drive or external source.

INTEGRATED CIRCUIT   A complete electronic circuit, reduced and imprinted onto a semiconductor surface.

INTERPRETER   A term used to describe that section of program which translates high level language into machine language.

INTERRUPT   A signal sent from a peripheral device to the computer which is understood to be a request for service routines.

KEYBOARD   This word describes the push buttons used to enter ASCII characters into the computer.

KEYFIELD   Part of a record used in search operations to locate the correct record for updating.

KEYWORD   Usually the first word after a line number, e.g. PRINT GOTO etc. Also can be applied to the first identifying word in a data file used for search purposes.

KILO   Thousand, 10K Bytes = 10,000 Bytes. Often pronounced 'K' (Kay).

LANGUAGE

The codes the computer understands. Languages can be divided into three sections - high level languages by which we mean BASIC, FORTH etc. These are close to English and are therefore understood by both human beings and computers. Low level languages such as Assembler use short phrases (mnemonics) which usually suggests the word they represent i.e. LDY = Load, register Y. The third is Machine Code which is presented to the machine as Hexadecimal (Hex).

L.E.D.

Light Emitting Diode.

LOAD

Load has two meanings. The first is the act of bringing information into the computer from the storage medium. The second means lower the head onto the disk surface on a floppy disk drive. (Unloaded is to hold the head away from the disk).

LOGIC

The relationship between events expressed in mathematical terms.

LOOP

A series of instructions which are repeated a predetermined number of times.

MACHINE CODE

Sometimes referred to as machine language, means in effect binary digits contained within the memory area when presented to the human operators. Higher languages are generally used.

MAGNETIC FIELD

The area of magnetic flux surrounding a magnetic or electromagnetic object.

MEGA	One million, 1M Bytes means 1 million bytes.
MENU	A list of options within a program or a list of programs, arranged to accept your choice by keyboard entry of a variable.
MICROCOMPUTER	A computer in which the central processing unit is contained within an integrated circuit, usually the microprocessor.
MICROPROCESSOR	An integrated circuit (chip) which performs the calculations and controls most of the other devices within a microcomputer.
MISMATCH	An error message produced when the computer expected a string and received a numeric variable or vice versa.
MNEMONICS	A system of abbreviations conserving memory space and used as tokens to represent larger words.
MULTI-STATEMENT LINE	A program line containing more than one command or statement, each separated from the others by a colon.
NUMERIC	Pertaining to numbers (not alphabetic) - see also Alphanumeric.

OPCODES

Codes containing operating instructions for a microprocessor.

OPERATING SYSTEM

The software provided with the computer usually contained in ROM and written in Machine Code which performs the routines demanded by higher level languages.

OUTPUT

Information fed out of the computer to other external devices such as a VDU or Printers.

PAGE

The information required to fill one TV screen. Page is also understood to mean the start address of user random access memory on a BBC Computer.

PAGE MODE

Stops the listing of a program on a VDU in order that each screenful can be read by the user. On the BBC Computer, page mode is invoked by CTRL/N and removed by CTRL/O. The page on view is updated each time the SHIFT key is pressed.

PAGED ROMS

A series of Read Only Memory devices, sharing the same address area and selected by software control, the address range on the BBC Computer being &8000 to &BFFF.

PLATTER

See disk.

PRESTEL

The name given to a database which can be called using your domestic telephone. Introduced by British Telecom. The American equivalent is known as Source.

PROCEDURE   Describes a subroutine that the computer can call without giving a line number i.e. PROCdump would transfer the action to an area of a program defined by DEFPROCdump and the action would be restored to its original place at the end of the procedure, shown by ENDPROC.

PROGRAM   A sequentially numbered list of instructions (noun). The act of entering a list of instructions into a computer (verb).

PROGRAM COUNTER   An area within the microprocessor which contains the address of the next program line to be executed.

RAM   Random Access Memory. An area of memory into which the microprocessor can write data or from which data can be read. It would perhaps be better to call this WARM (Write And Read Memory). Information contained in this area is lost when the computer is disconnected from the power supply.

RANDOM ACCESS   The ability to Read or Write information as required.

RECORD   Refers to a section of a file containing related alphanumeric and numeric information.

REGISTER   Used to describe memory areas within the microprocessor which contain address or data information about to be utilized by the CPU (Central Processing Unit).

RELATIVE

Used in conjunction with a predefined point, spaced from this point by a fixed numeric distance, e.g. memory address 0000 being a reference then &000A is + 10 (decimal) relative to 0000.

ROM

(Read Only Memory) Memory from which the microprocessor can read information but cannot change the information in any way. The information is fixed and is not affected when the computer is disconnected from the power supply.

SCROLLING

The act of adding an extra line on a terminal device causing all other lines to move one place in the opposite direction.

SEARCHING

Reading records sequentially until a keyfield is identified as belonging to the chosen records. Searching can also be understood to mean finding the program required on the disk.

SEARCH TIME

Indicates the time taken to locate information from one track to another, typically 6 ms.

SECTOR

Part of a track capable of holding 256 bytes.

SERIAL

A succession of information offered sequentially one bit at a time.

SIDEWAYS ROMS

See Paged Roms.

SOFTWARE

The program being used by the computer containing instructions and information.

SORTING

Placing information into a pre-arranged order e.g. alphabetically.

SPOOL	A program which is saved as ASCII tokens. This can be brought into the computer in a manner which will add the spool to another program in RAM using EXEC.
SUBROUTINE	An often - used part of a program, written as a separate section and containing an instruction at the end which returns the action to the program line after the one used to enter the routine.
TAPE	Cassette tape recording system.
TELETEXT	Textual information carried on a television signal. A special set is required to decode the information.
TOKEN	A symbol used to represent either data or commands. " ' " is equal to PRINT would make ' a token.
TRACK	The concentric ring of recorded information consisting of 10 sectors of 256 bytes. One disk surface can contain 80, 40 or 35 such tracks according to the make of drive.
TUBE	An input/output port used to communicate between dissimilar microprocessors.
UPDATE	Overwrite a record with current information.
VARIABLES	Combinations of letters and symbols which the computer assigns to either numbers or words. These are then known as numeric variables or string variables. String is indicated by the symbol $.

V.D.U.   Visual Display Unit. The device used to display pictorial information similar to and including televisions.

VECTOR   Memory locations used to contain an address which points to a usable subroutine usually in ROM. The address is typically 2 bytes long.

WALLET   The protective card case used to house a disk.

WILDCARD   Derived from the card game 'Poker', a multi-purpose symbol used in combination with other symbols to give the latter more power and flexibility, i.e. deuces wild means the playing card 2 can be taken to mean any value required.

WINDOW   The aperture through the wallet through which the head reads from or writes to the disk.

ZERO PAGE   A memory area whose address is &0000 to &00FF (256 bytes).

Index

185